ROSETTES 2

Scroll Saw Patterns

Marcus Clemons

This work is licensed under the Creative Commons Attribution-NonCommercial-NoDerivatives 4.0 International License. To view a copy of this license, visit http://creativecommons.org/licenses/by-nc-nd/4.0/ or send a letter to Creative Commons, 444 Castro Street, Suite 900, Mountain View, California, 94041, USA.

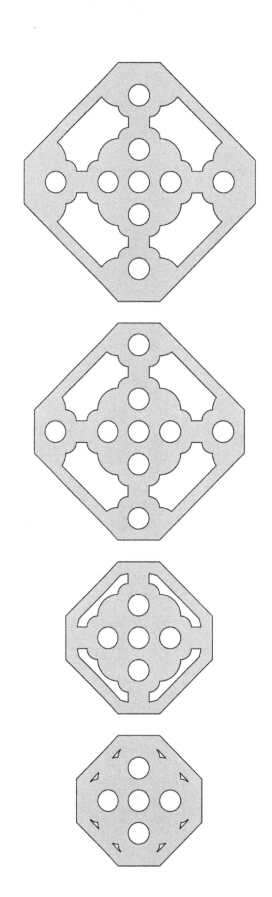

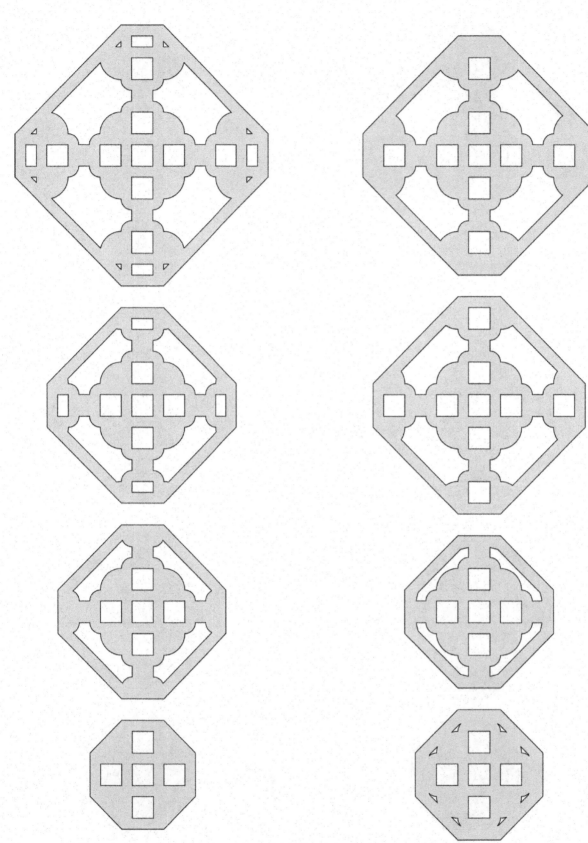

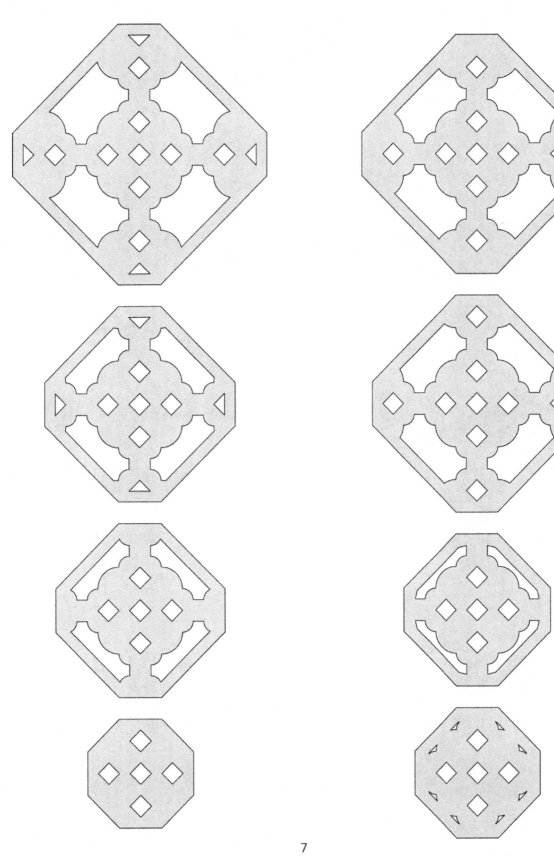

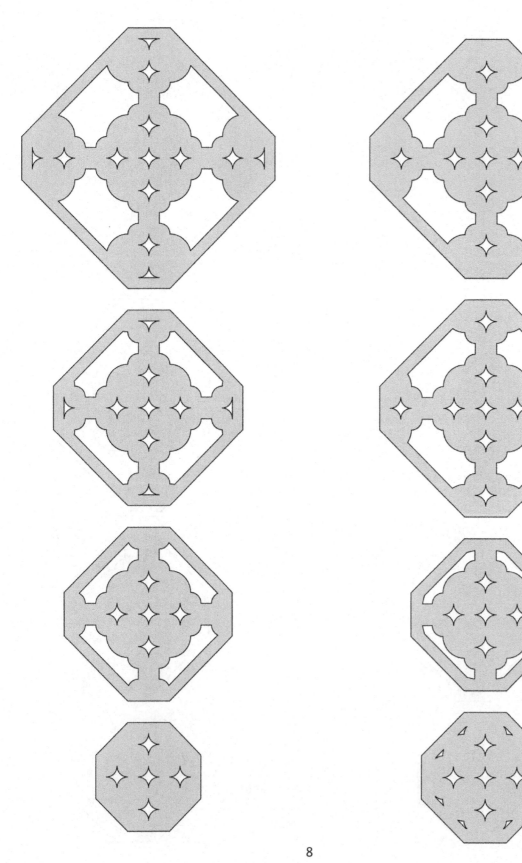

8

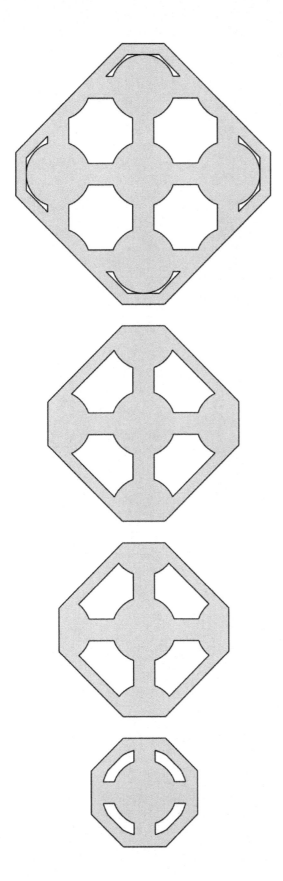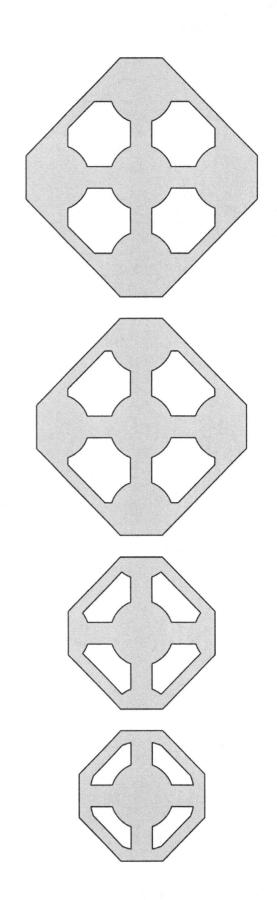

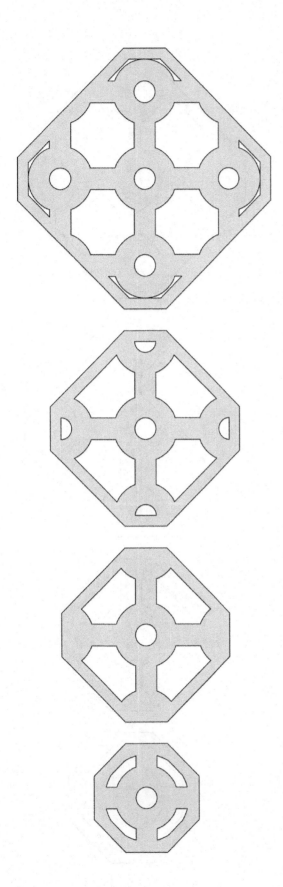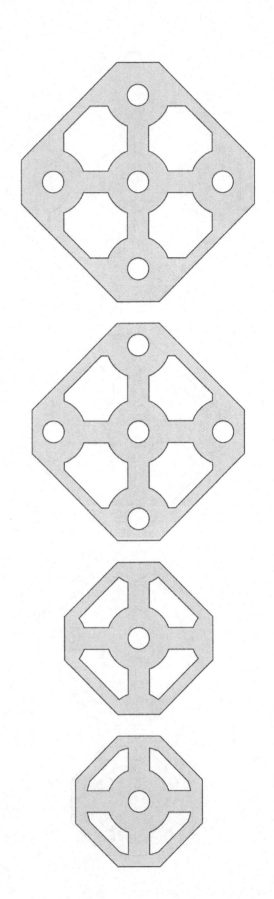

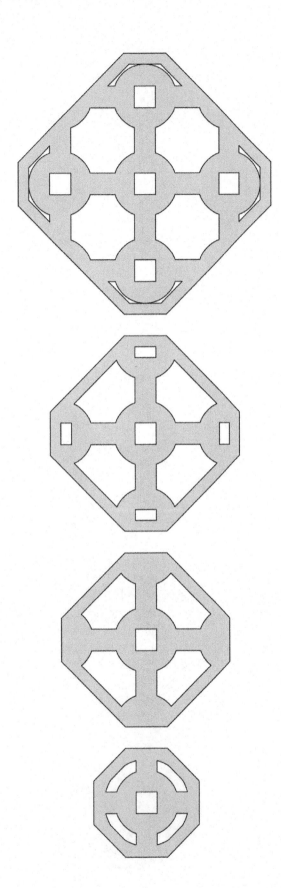
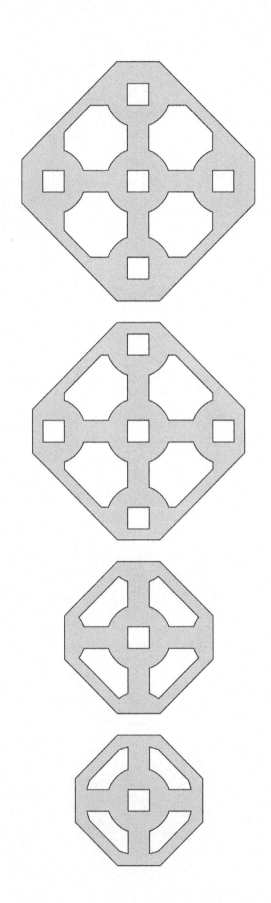

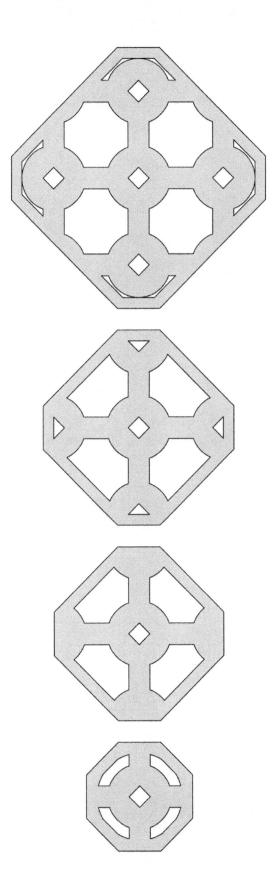
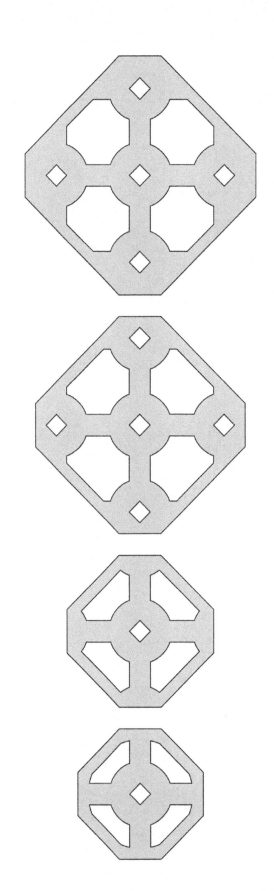

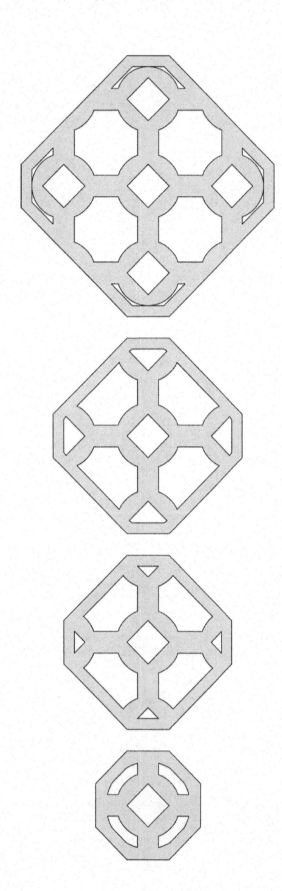
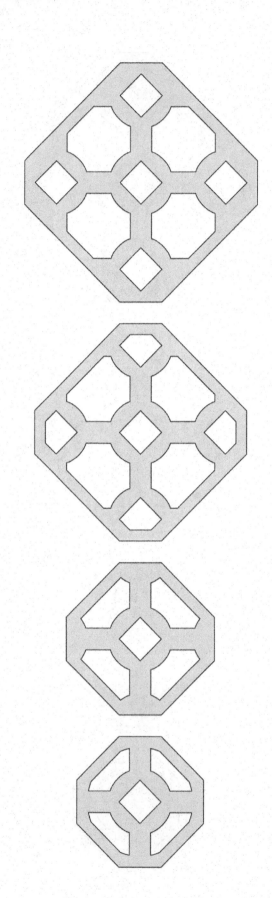

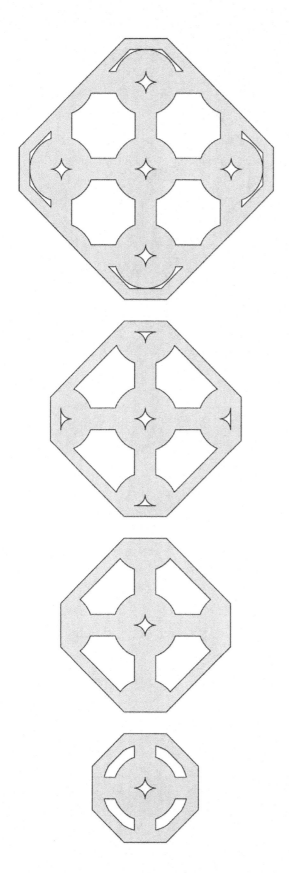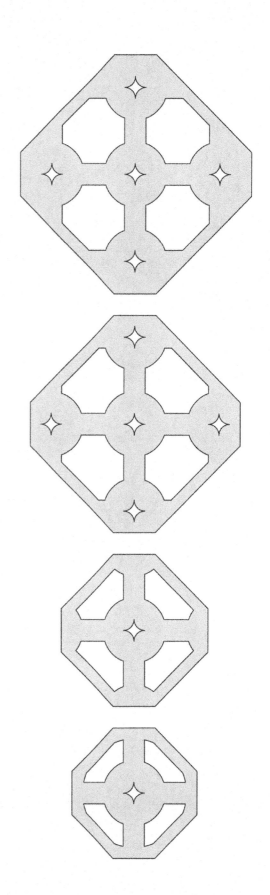

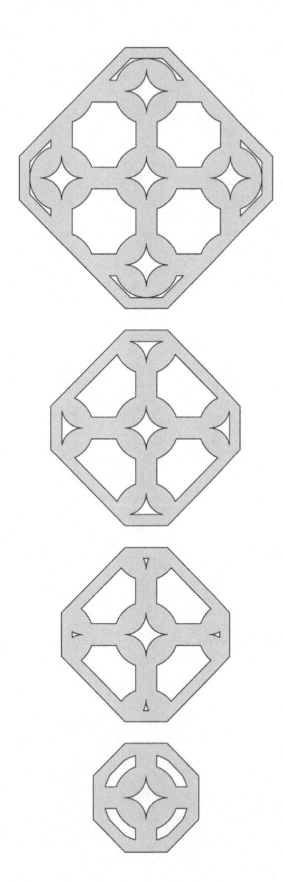
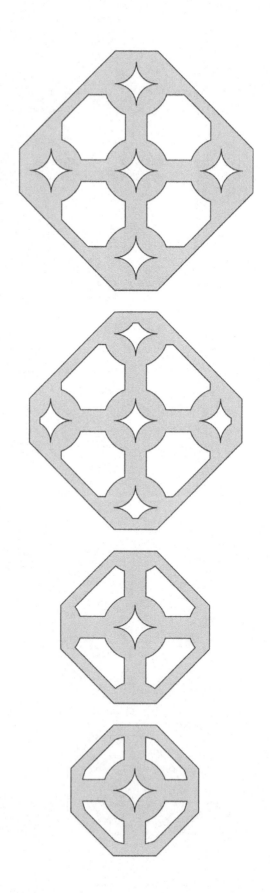

16

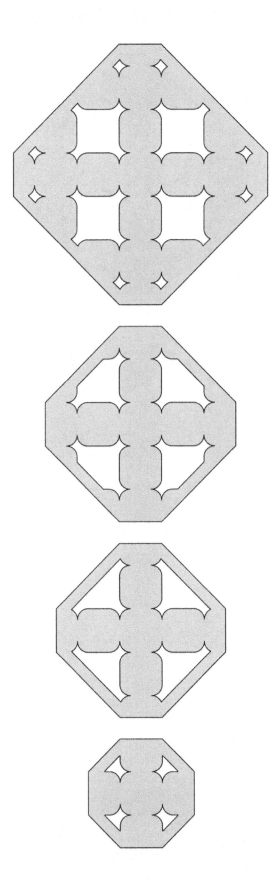
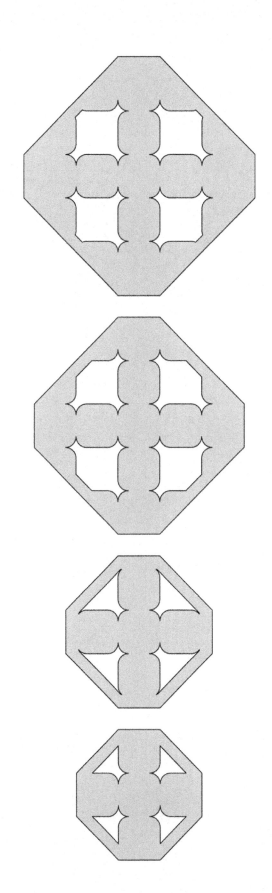

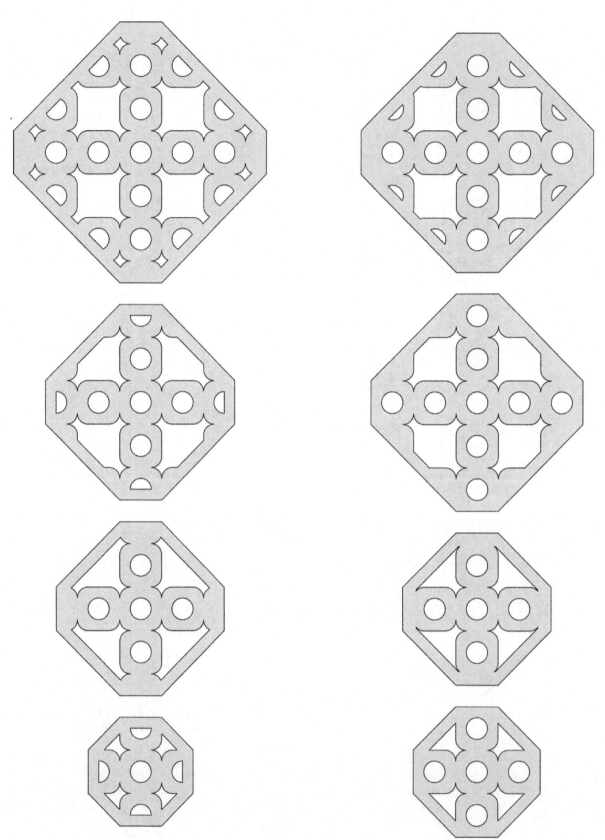

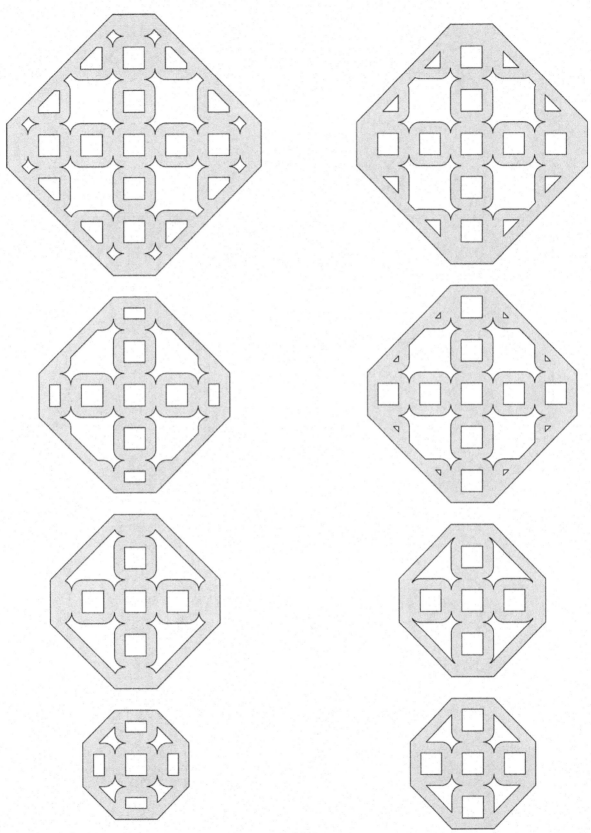

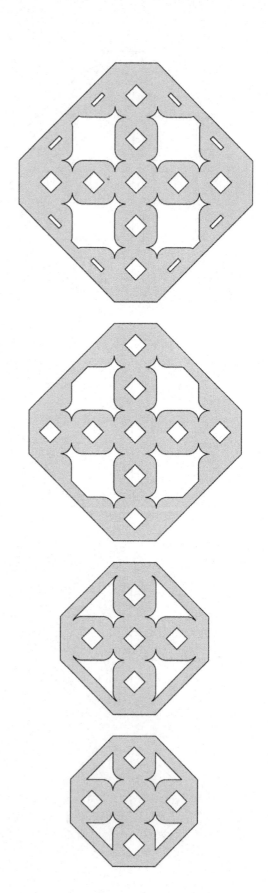

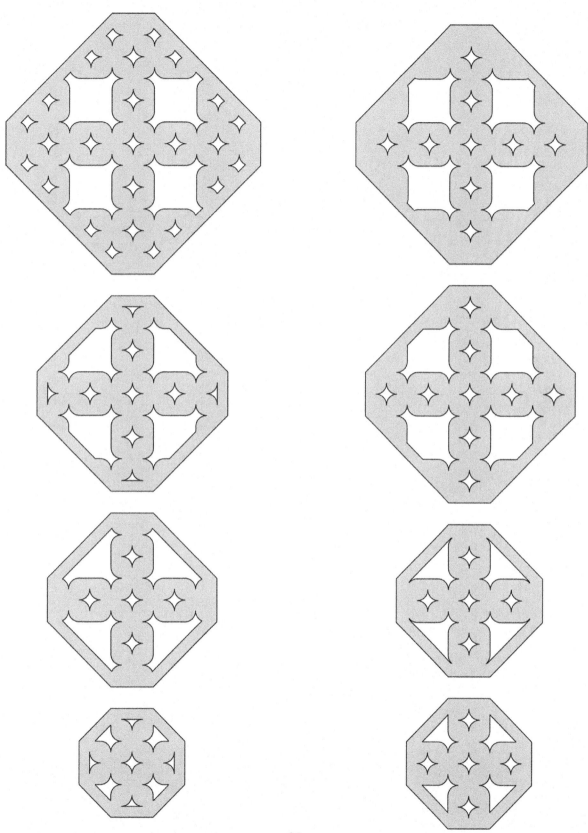

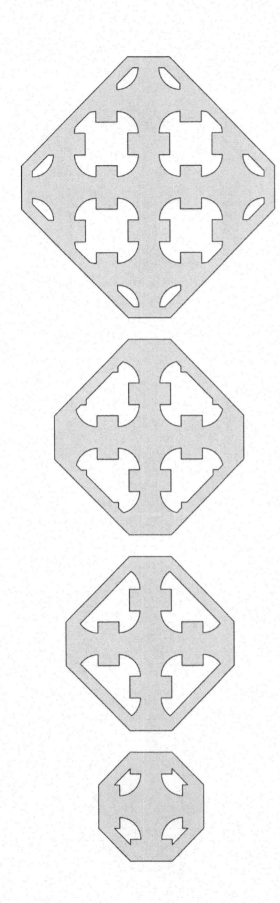
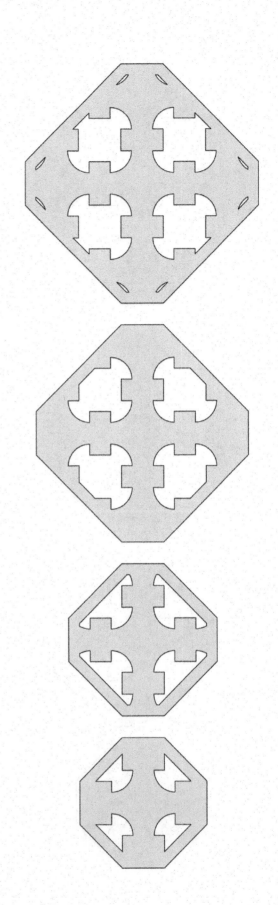

22

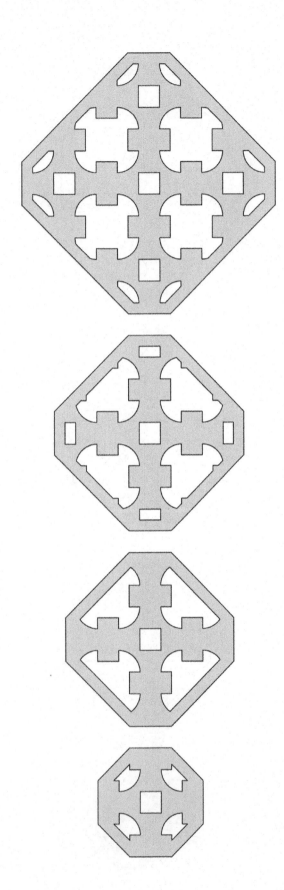
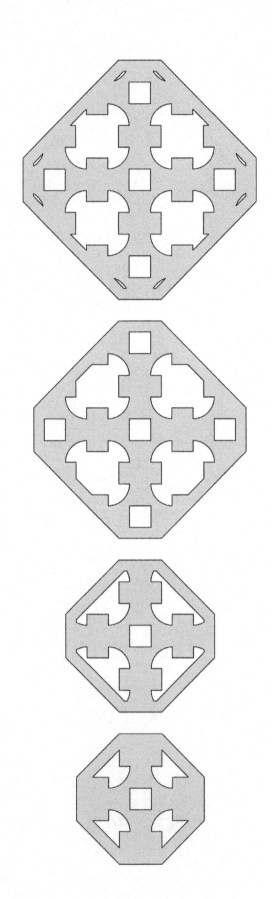

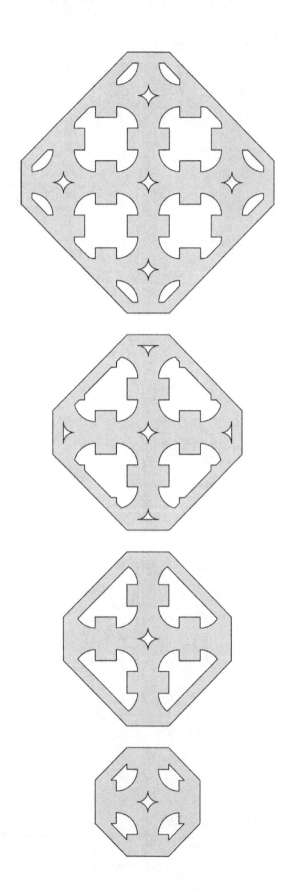
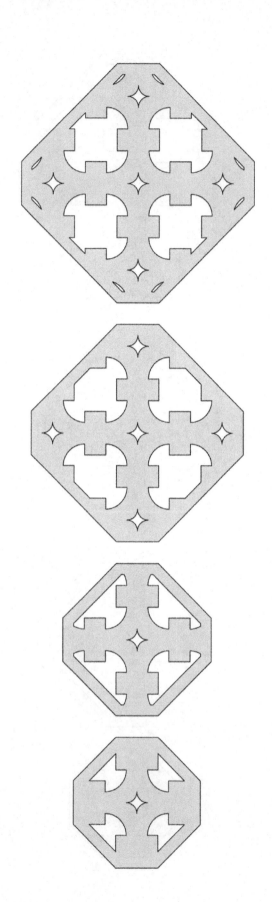

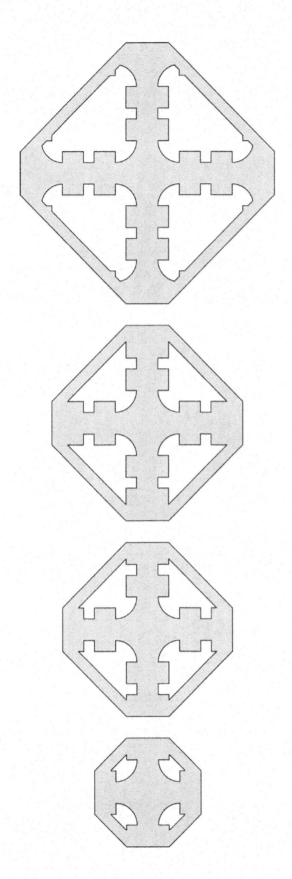
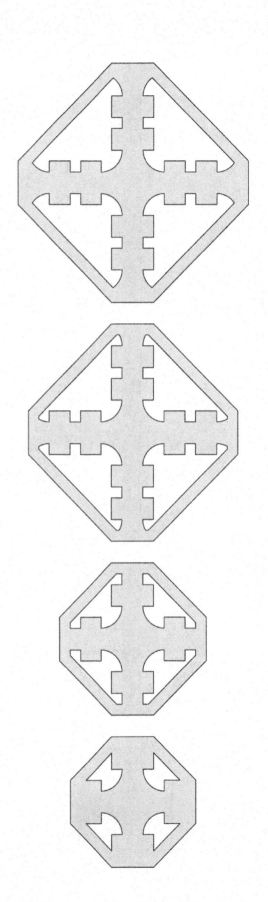

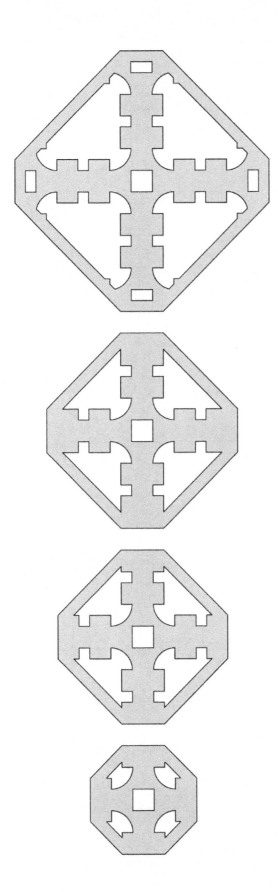

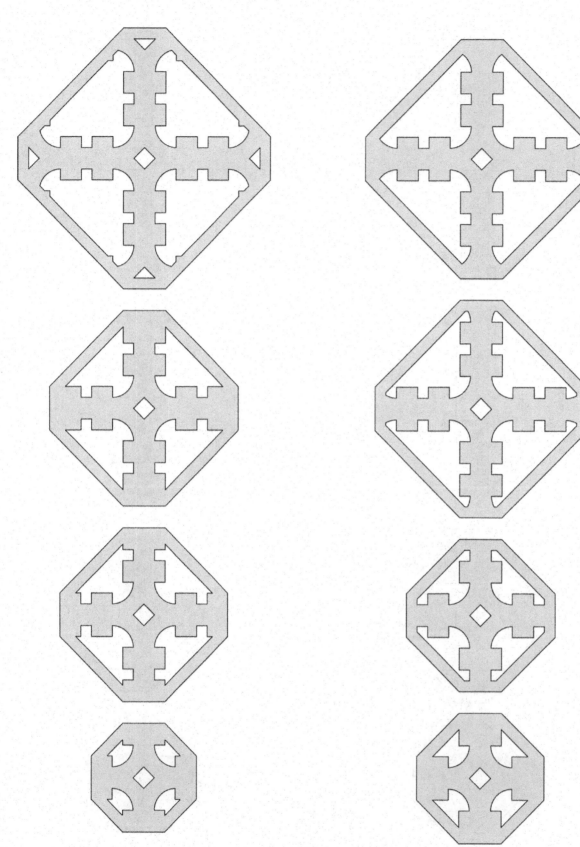

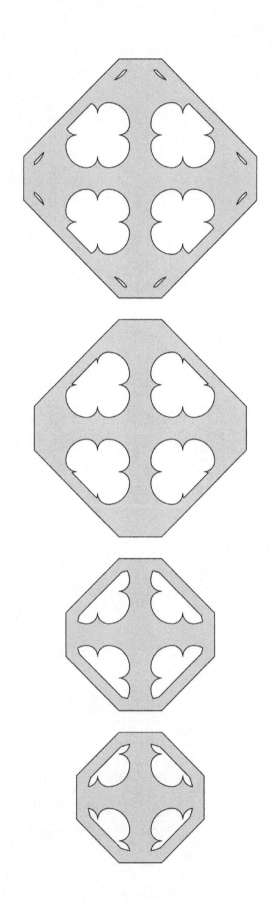

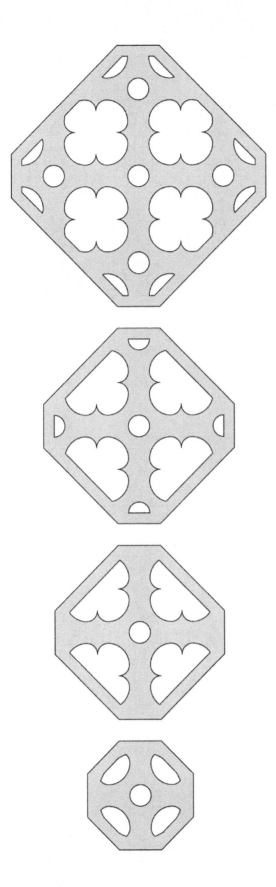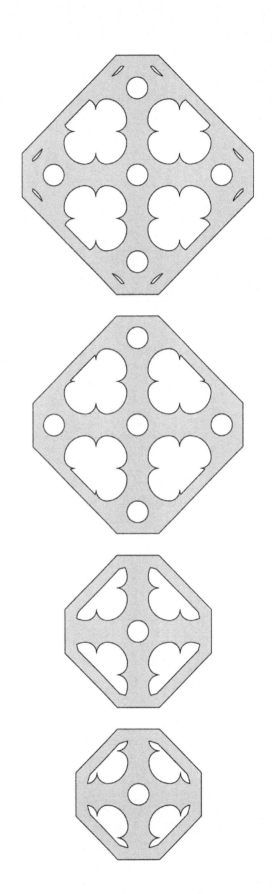

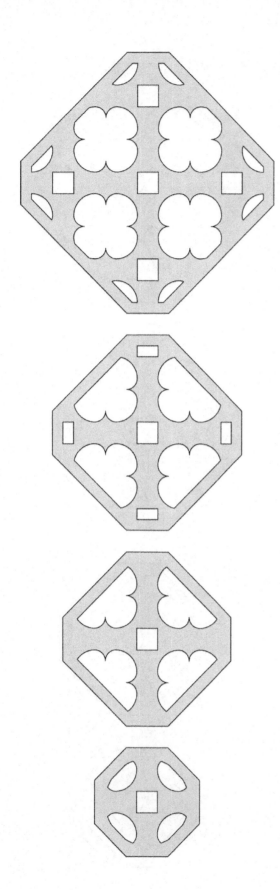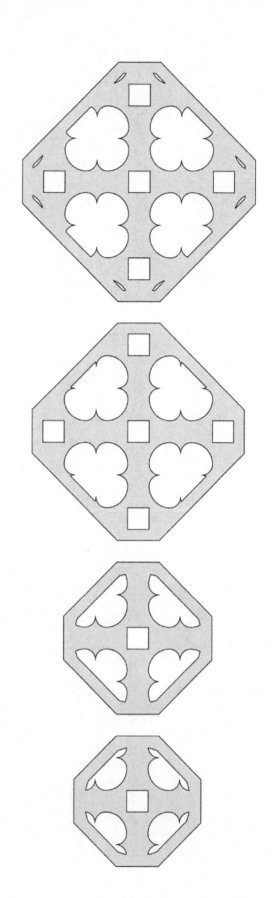

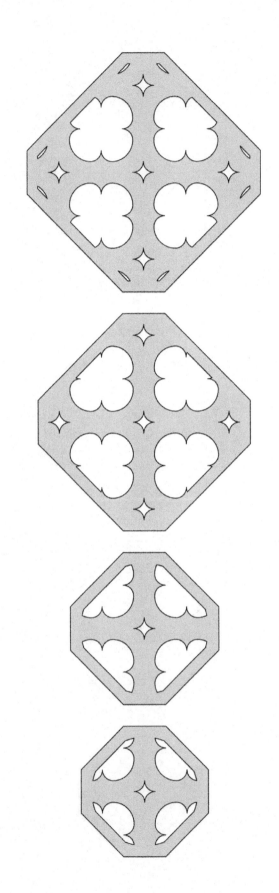

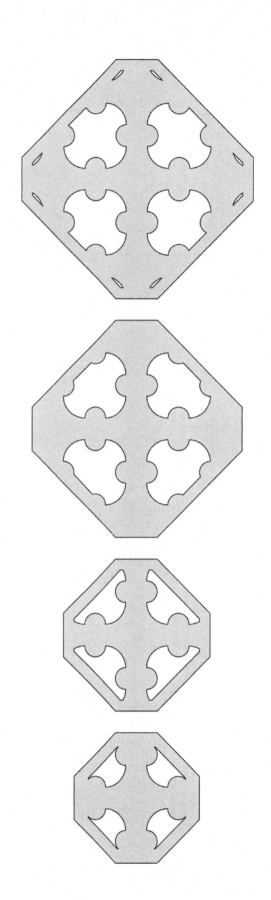

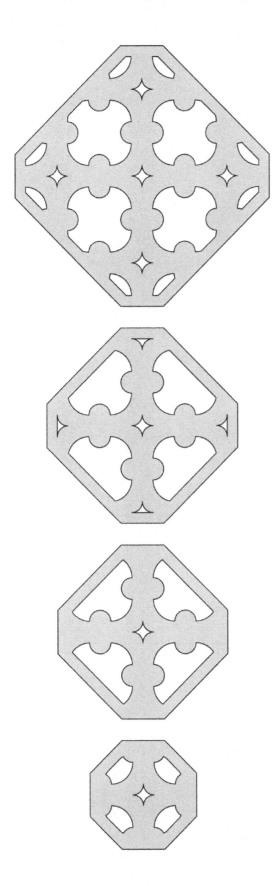

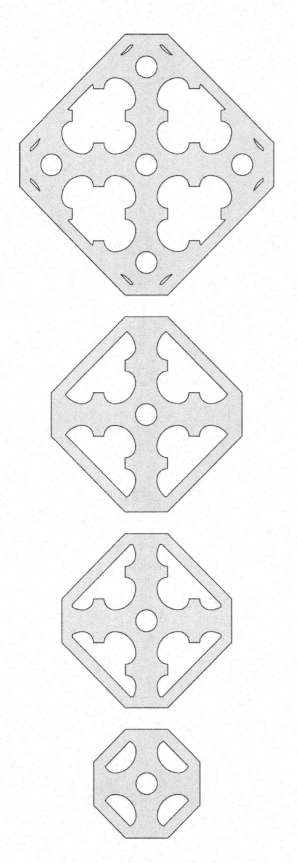
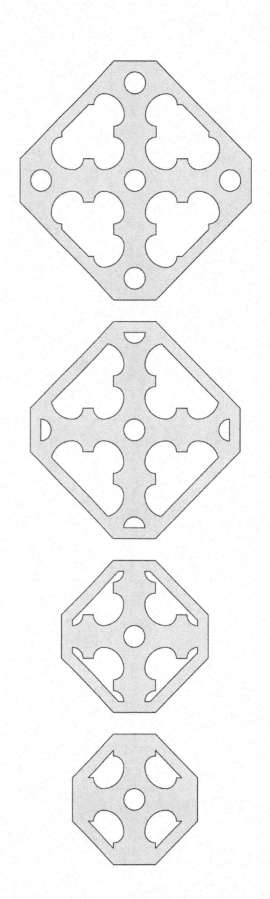

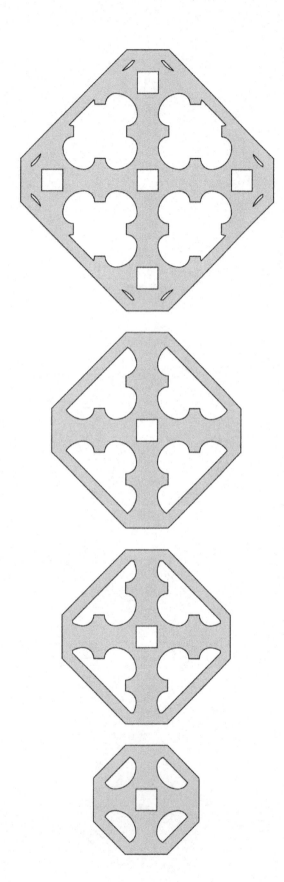
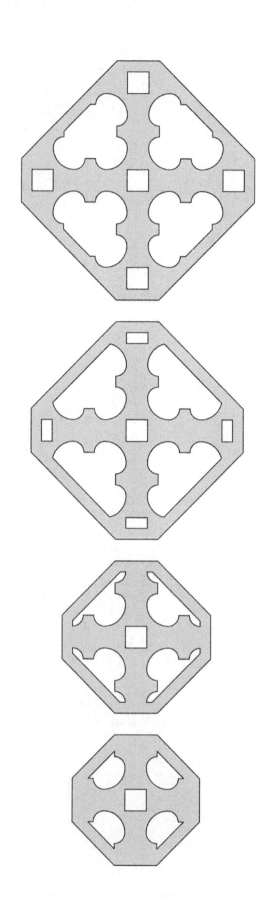

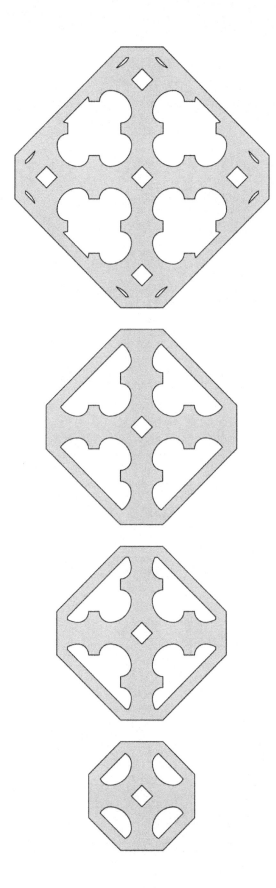

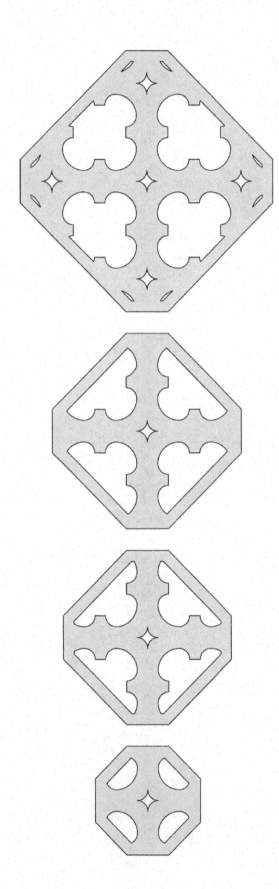

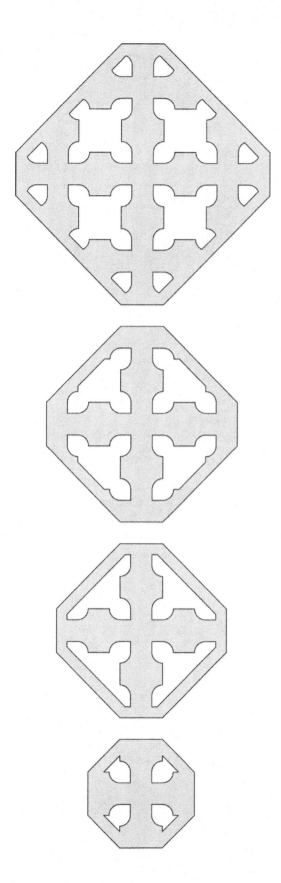
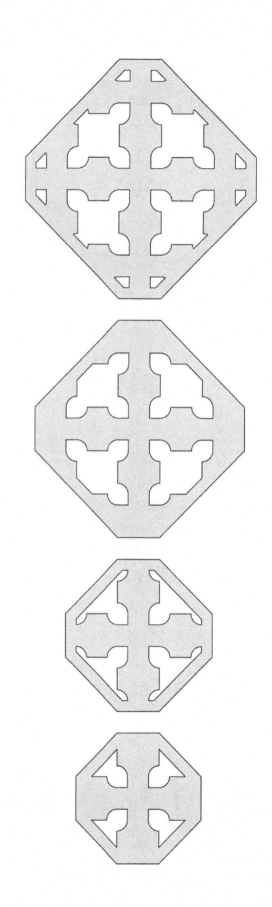

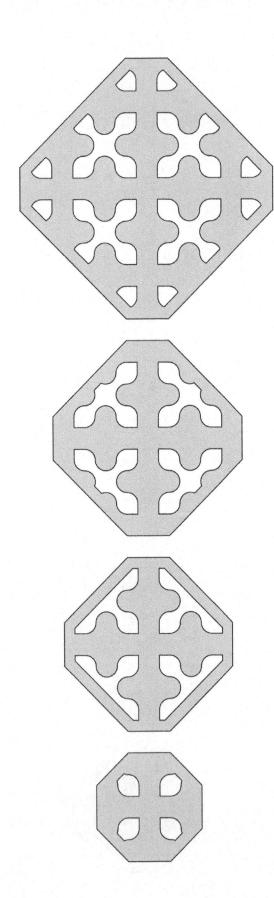
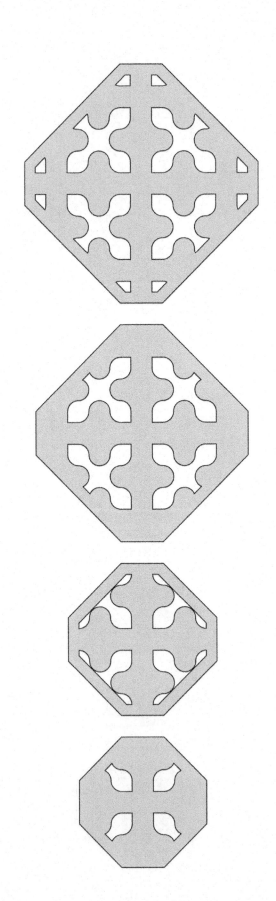

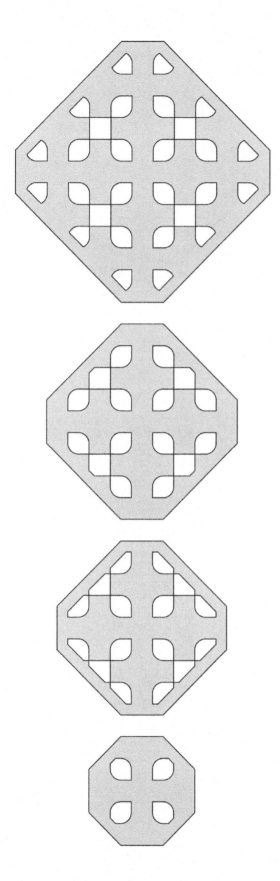
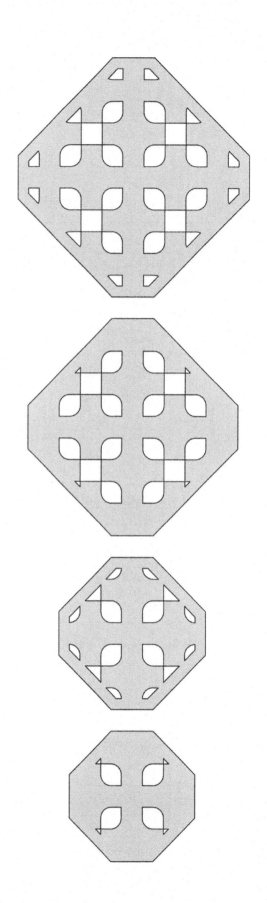

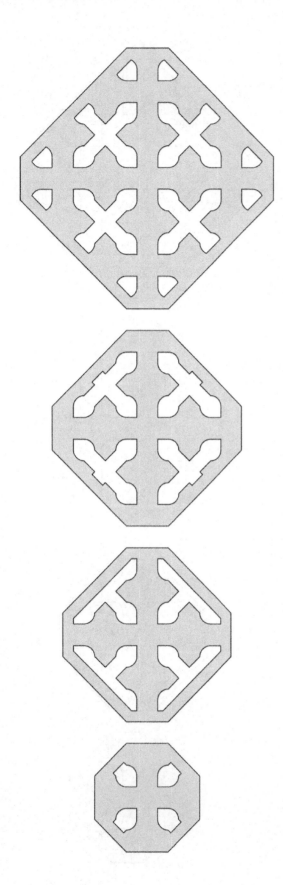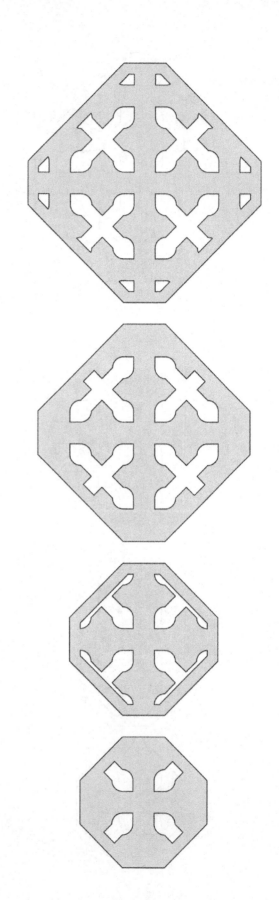

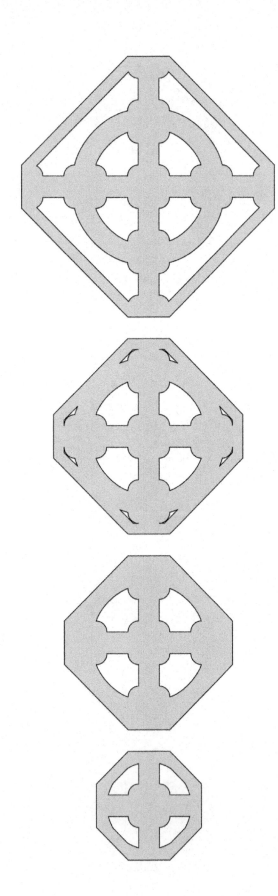

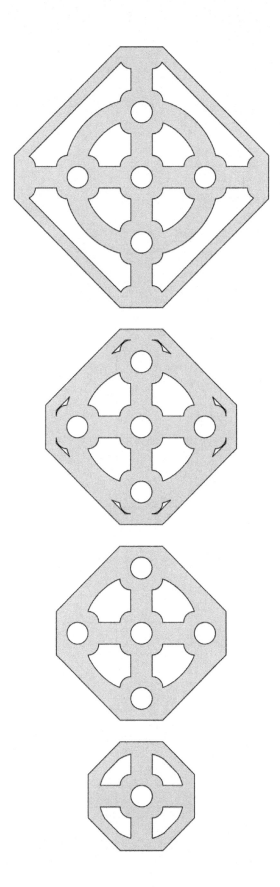

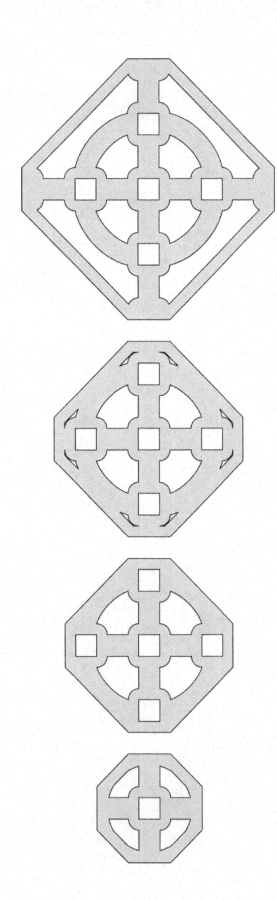
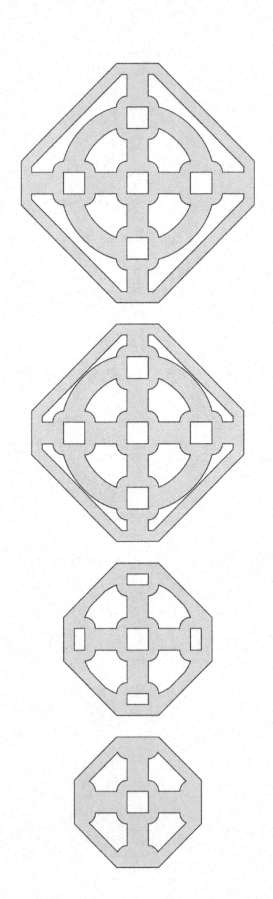

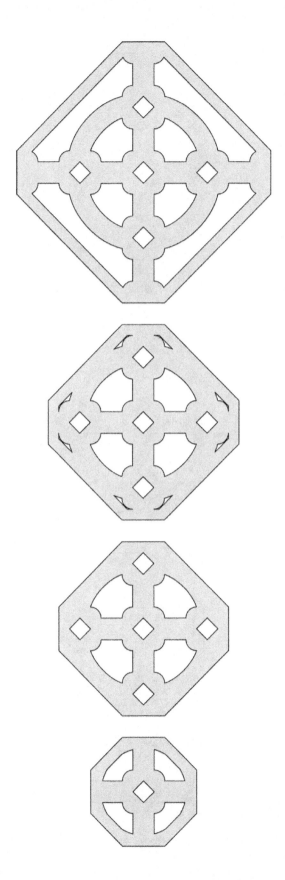

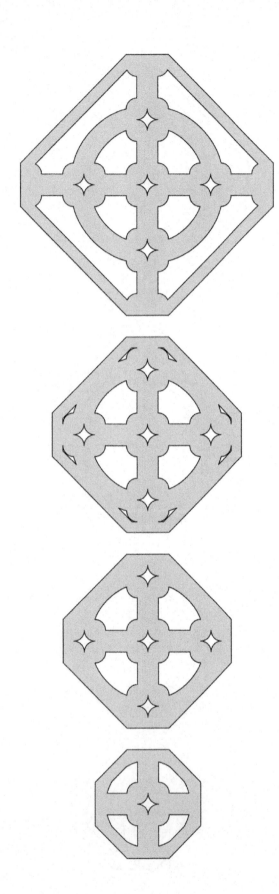

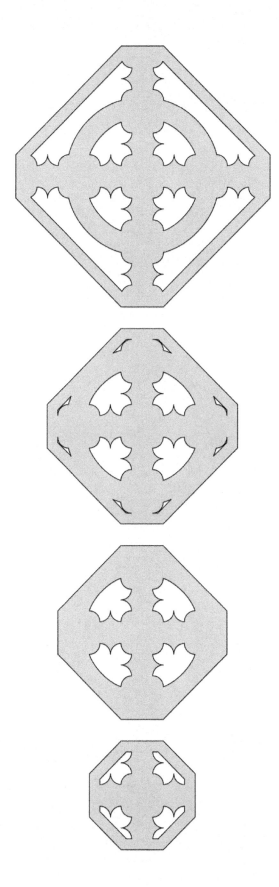
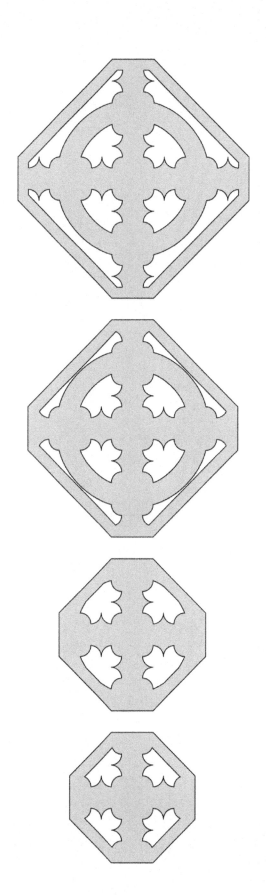

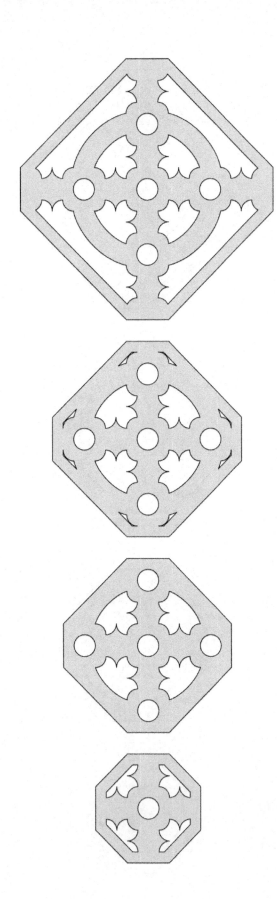

58

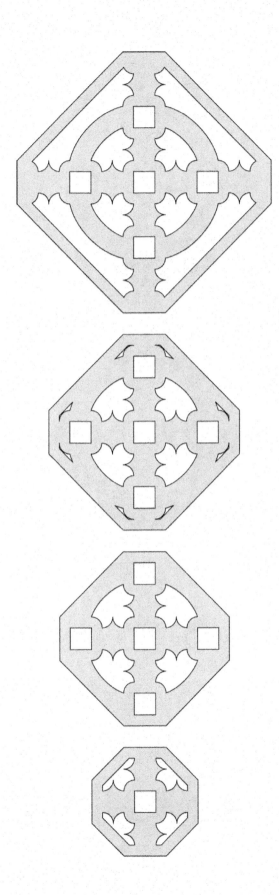
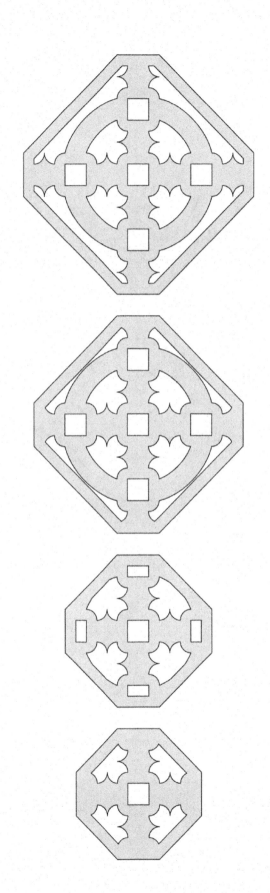

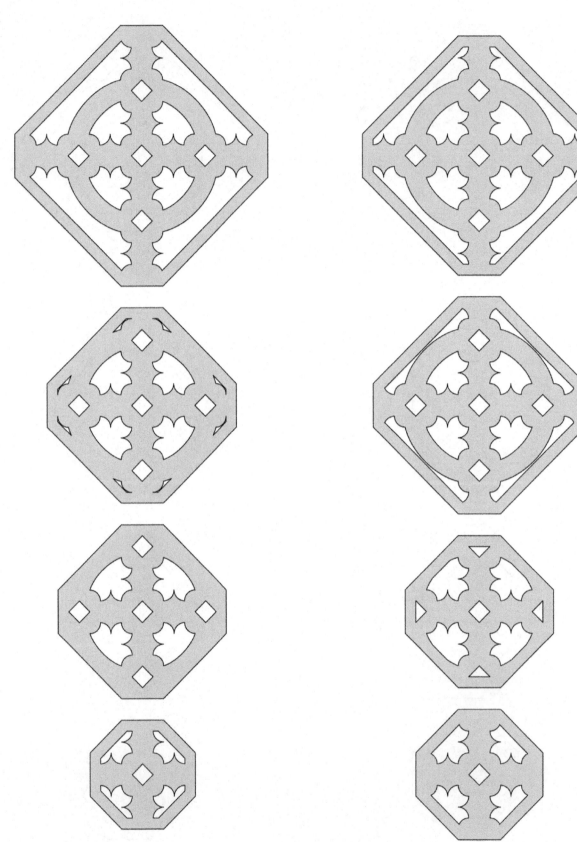

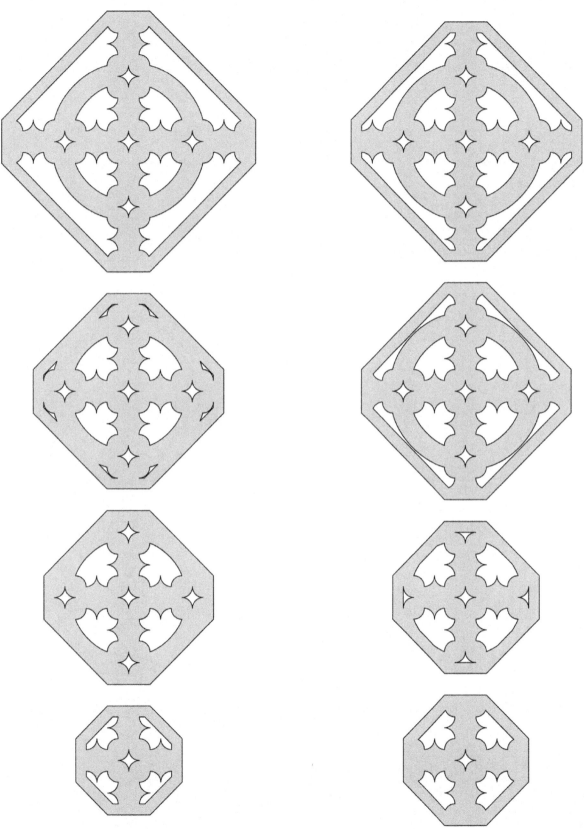

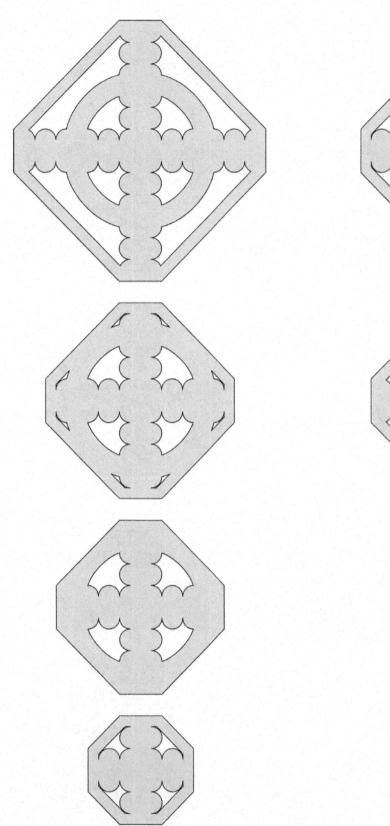

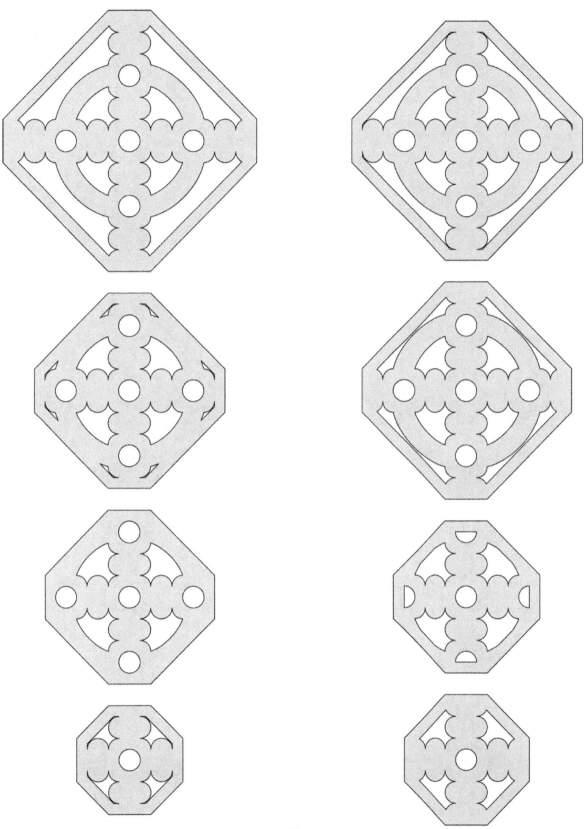

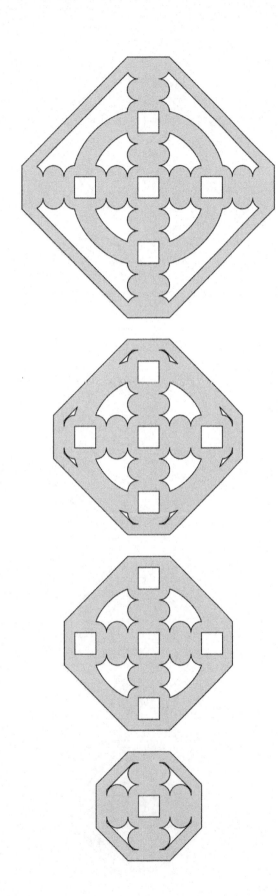
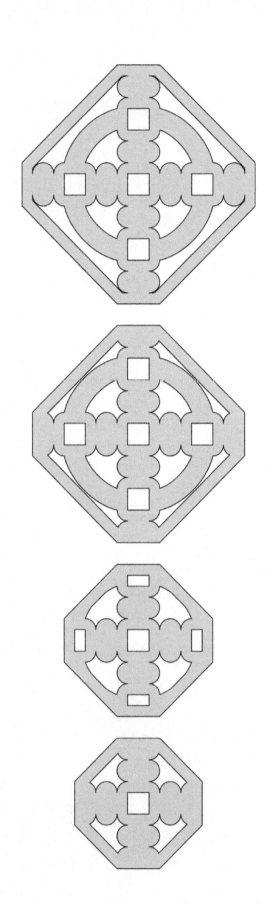

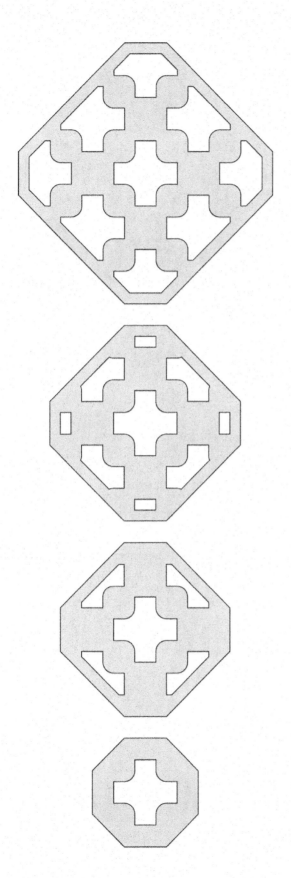

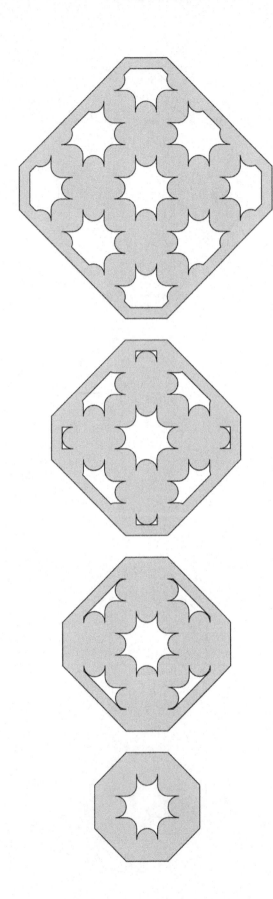

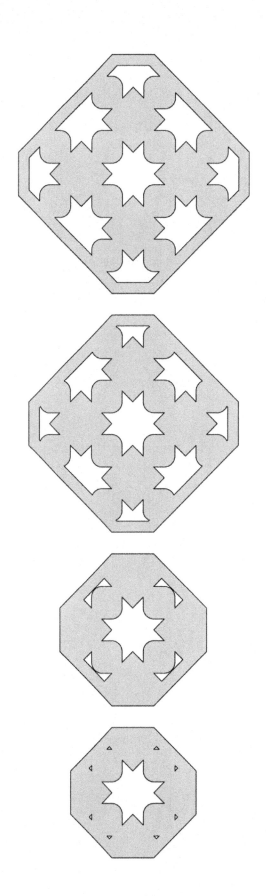

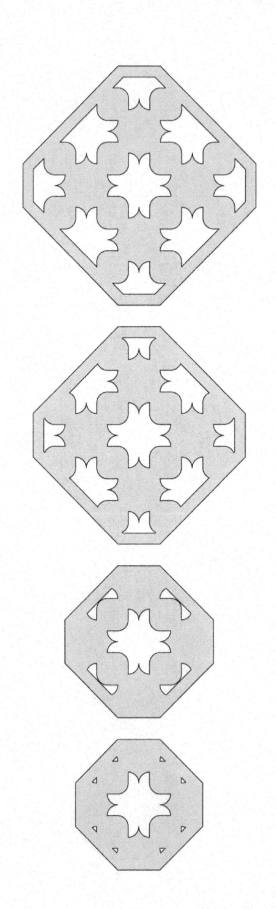

70

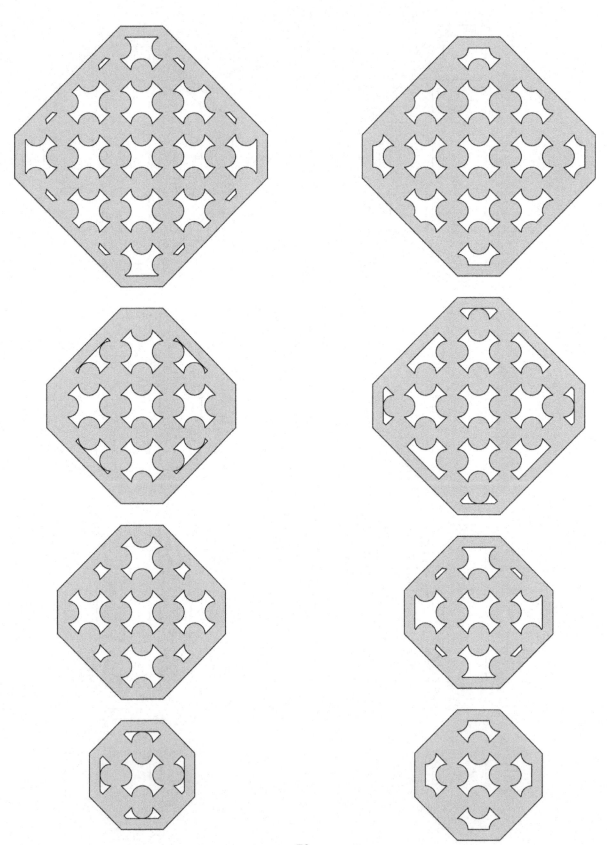

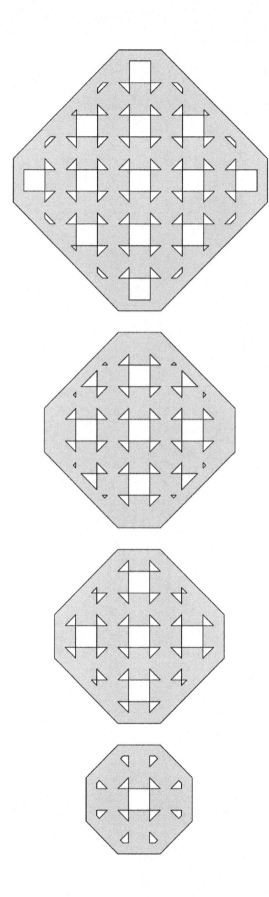
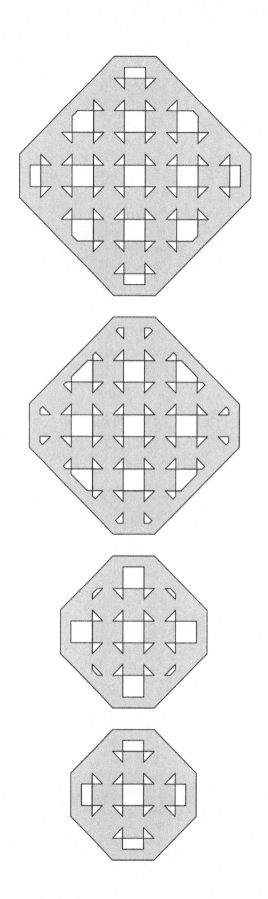

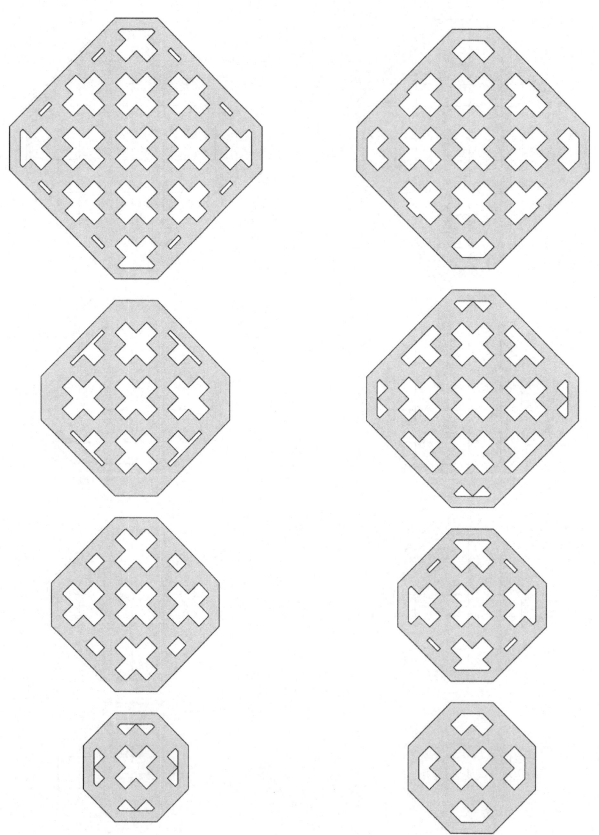

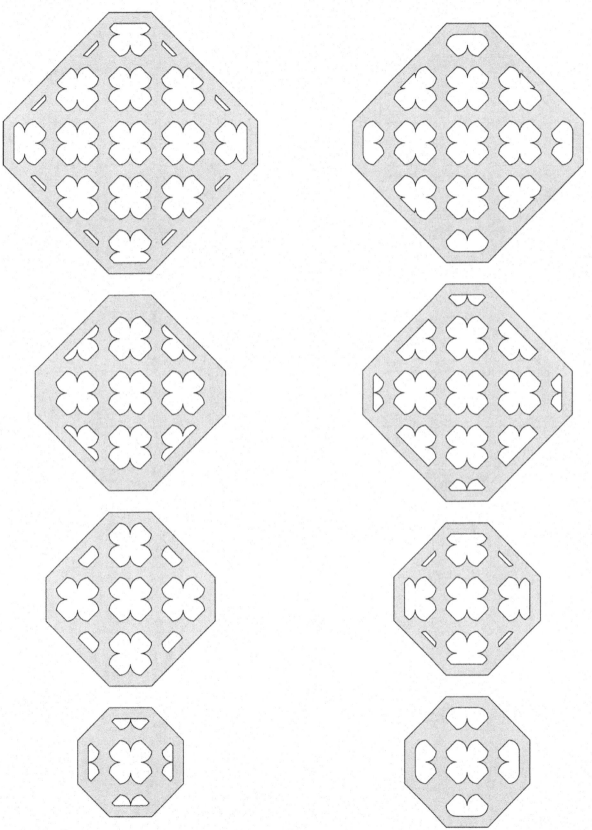

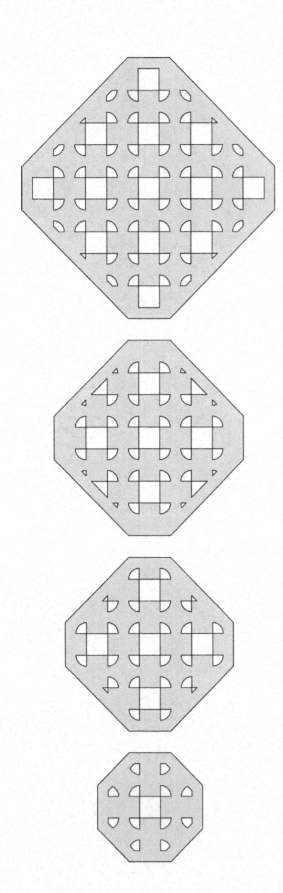
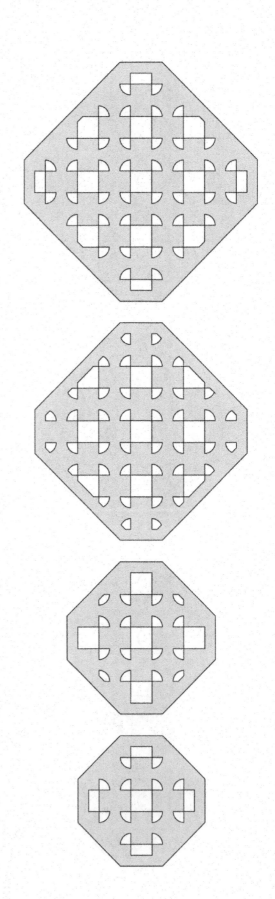

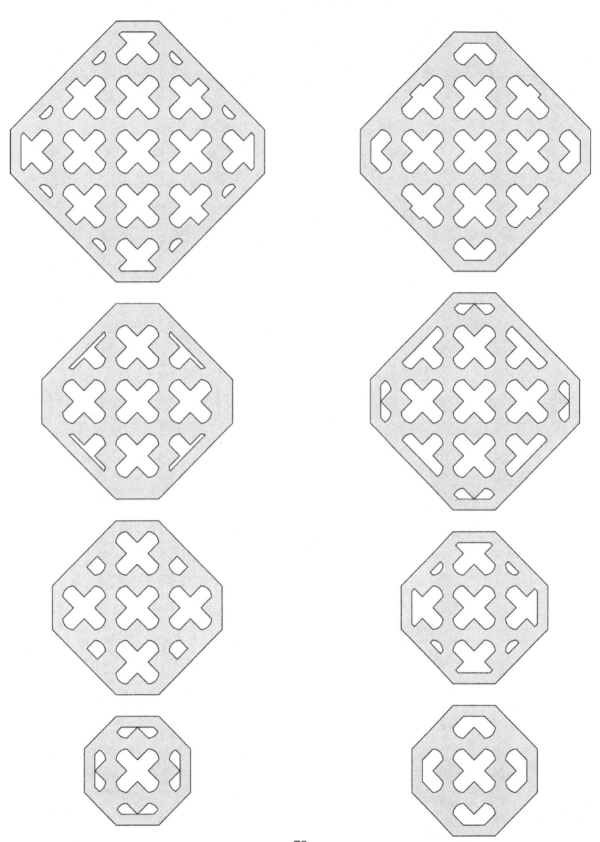

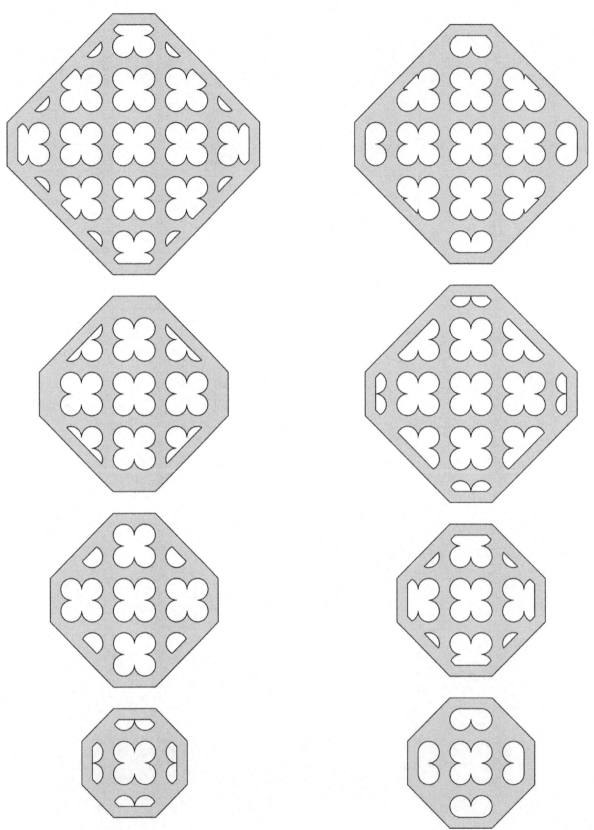

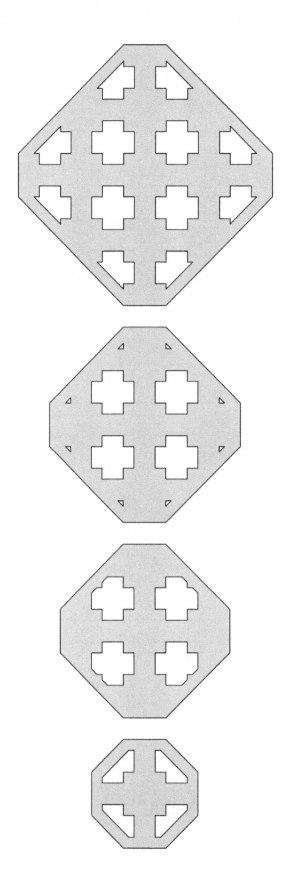
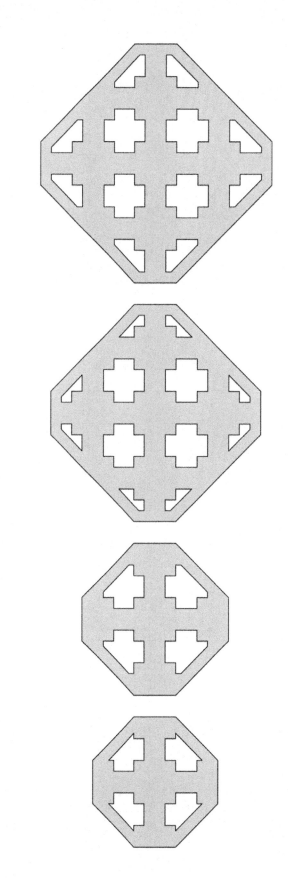

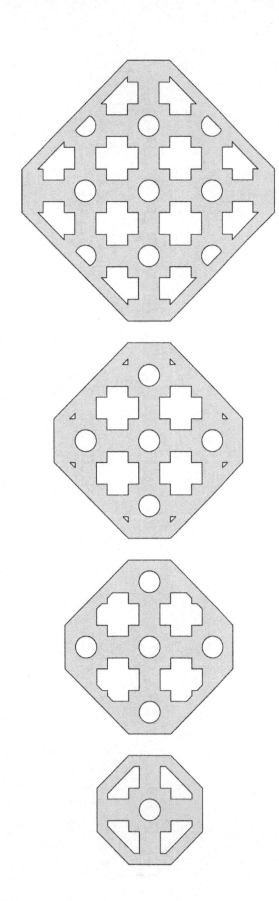

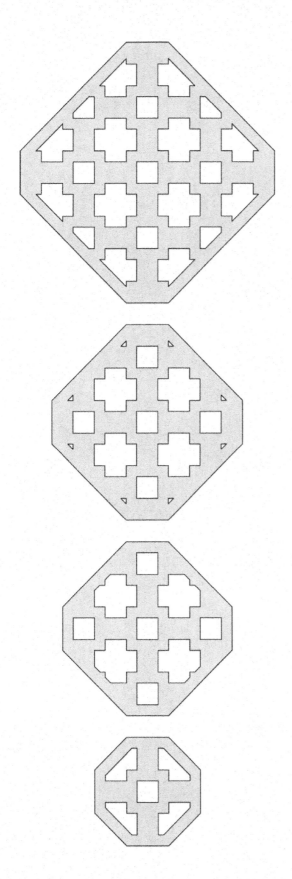
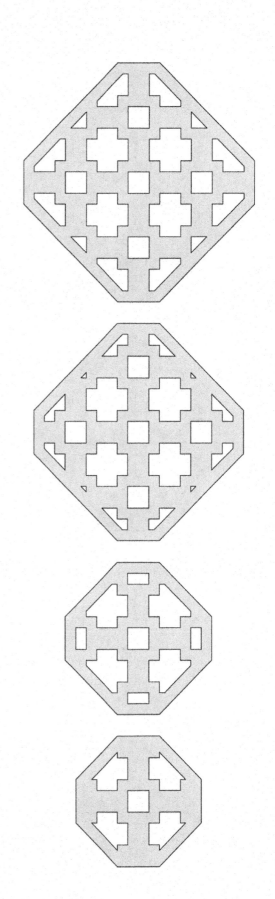

83

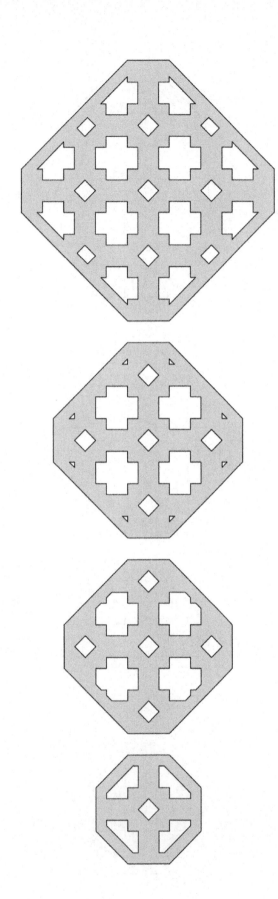

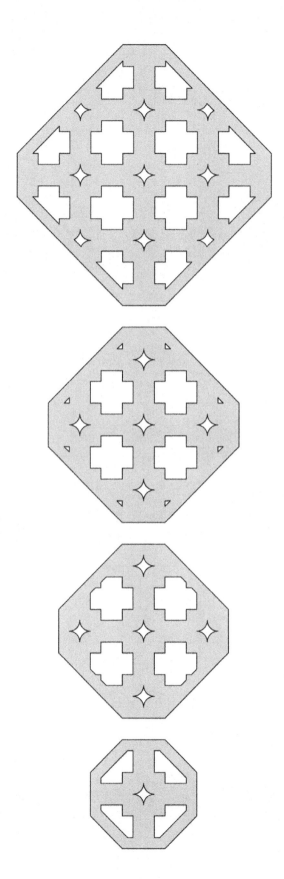

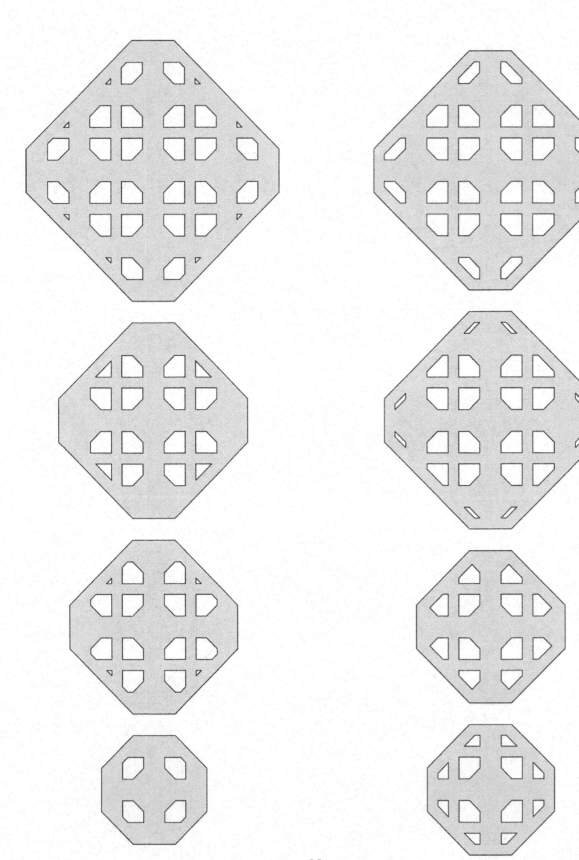

86

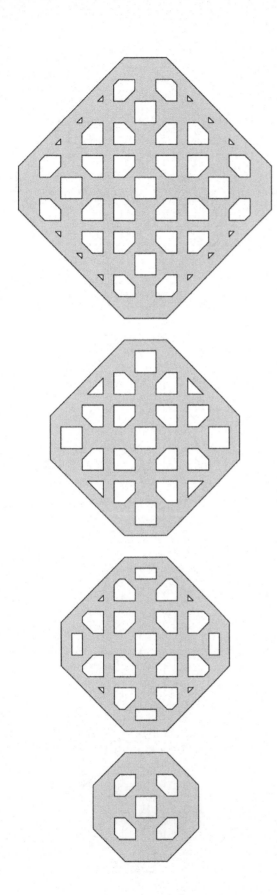
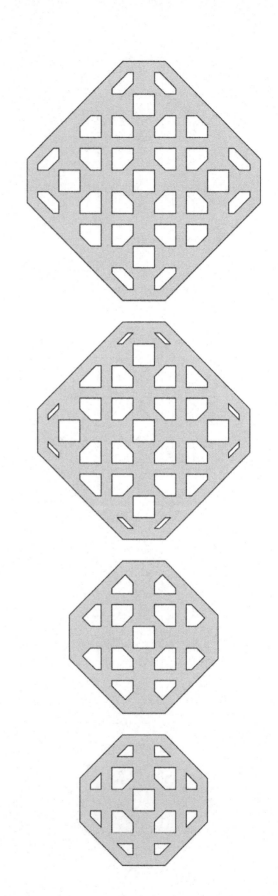

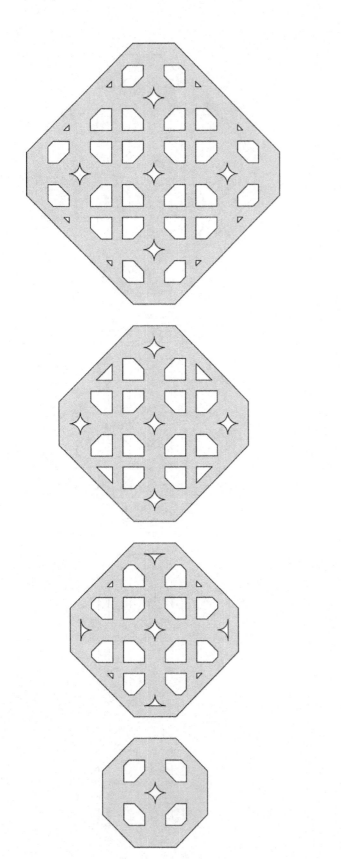

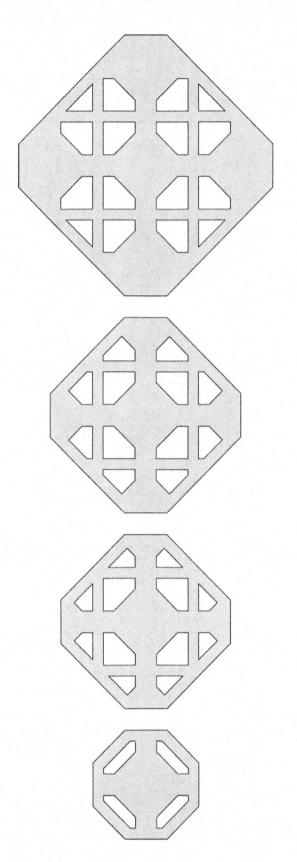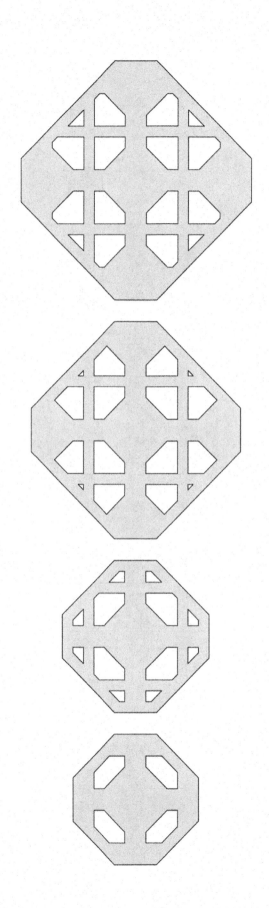

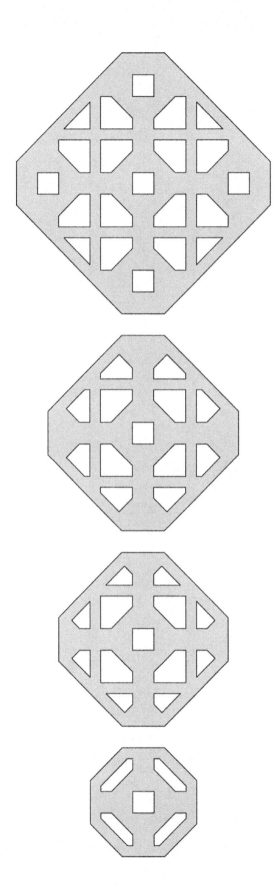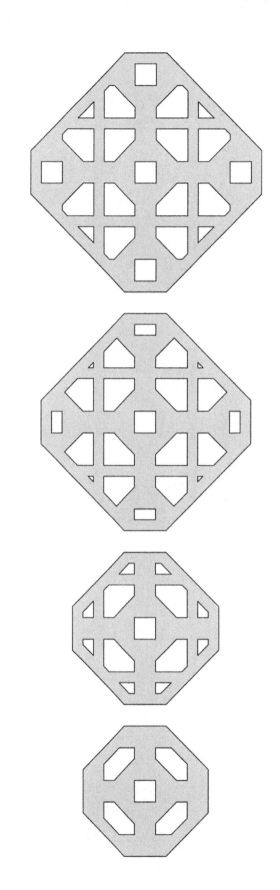

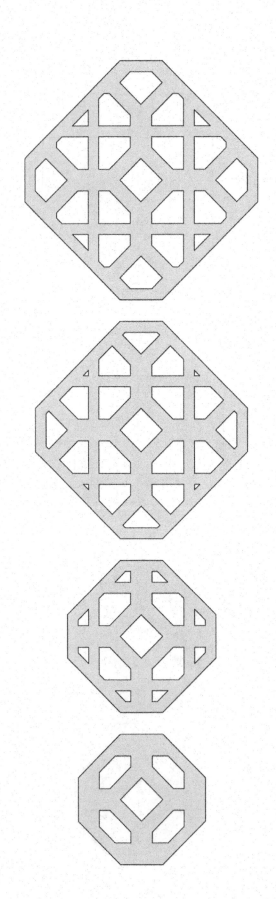

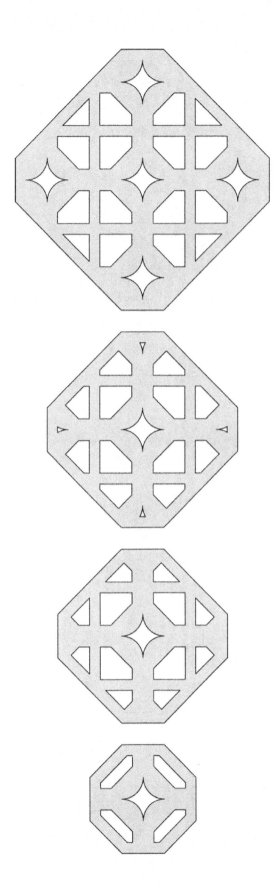

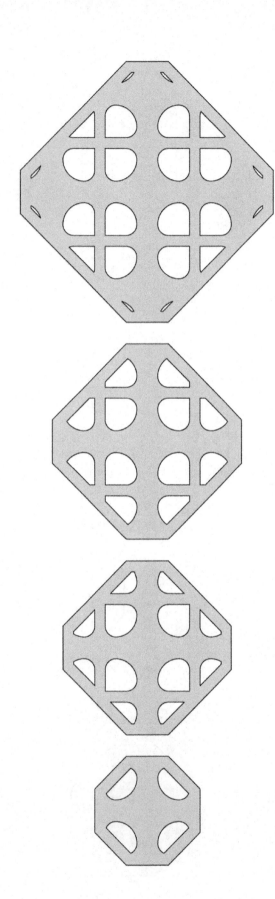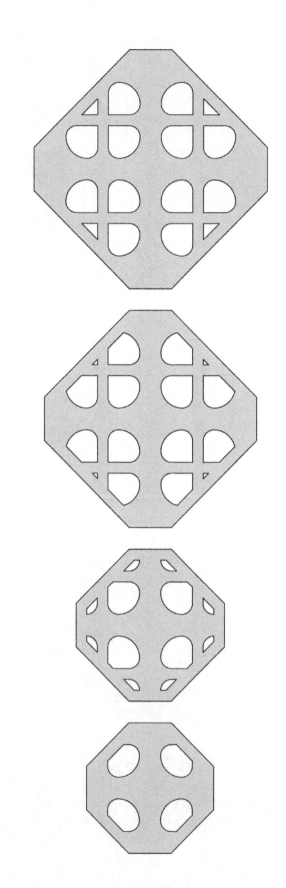

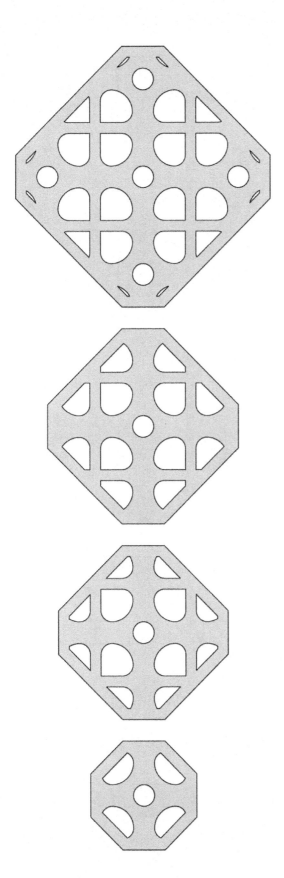
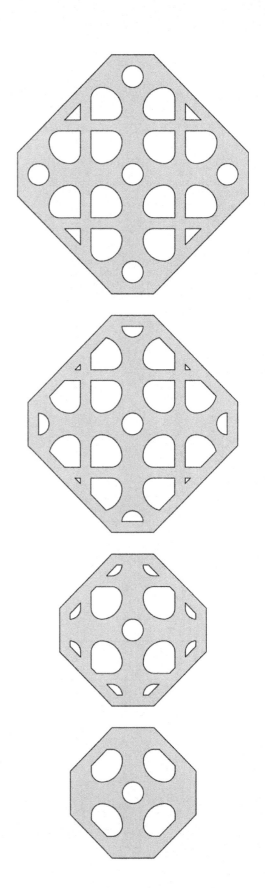

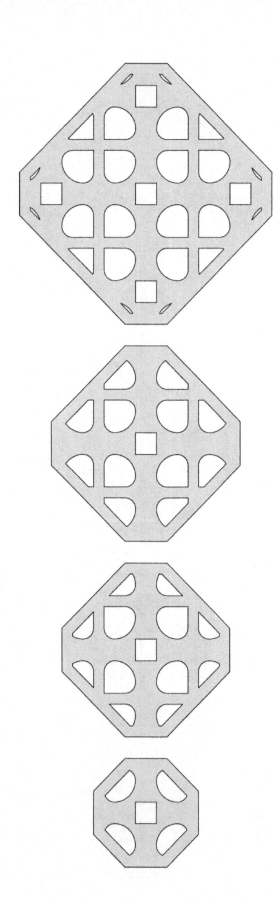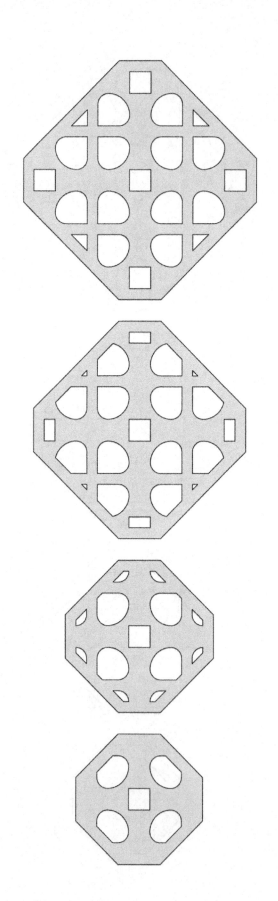

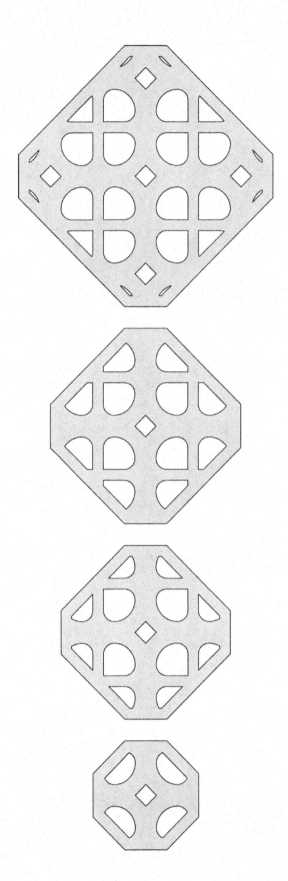
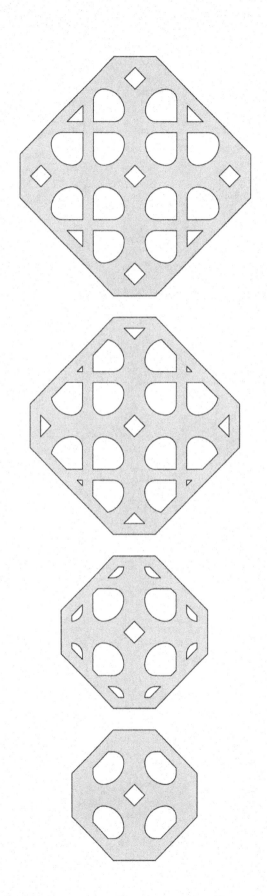

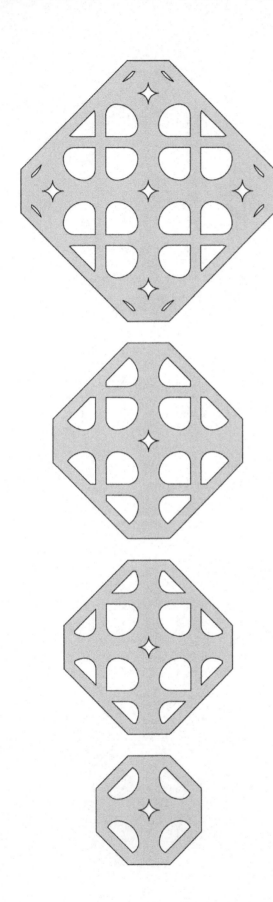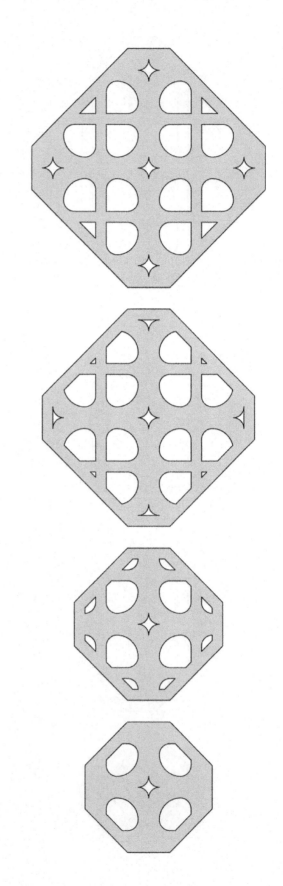

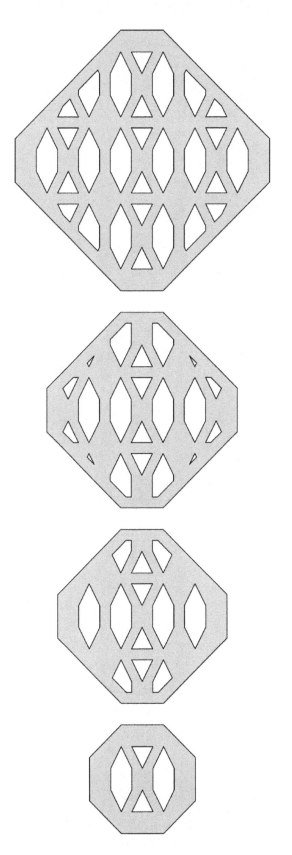
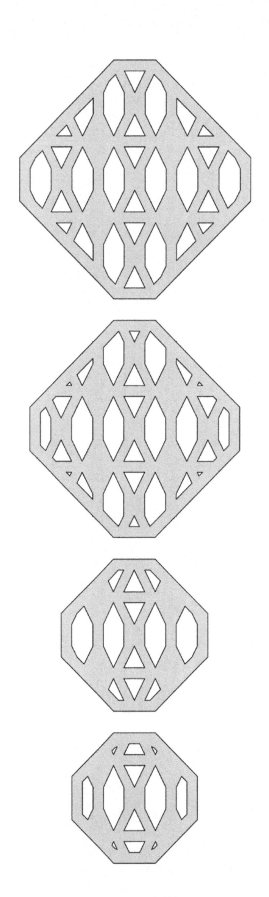

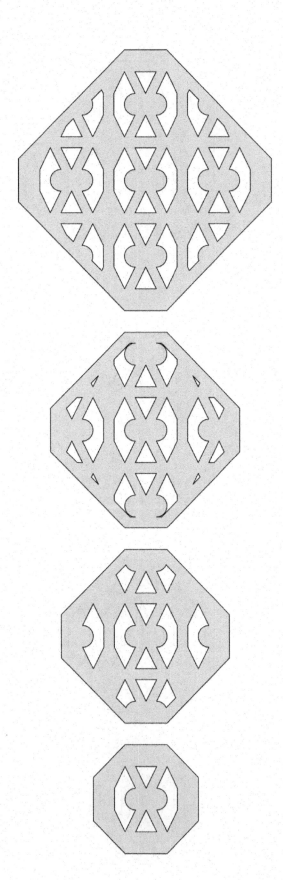
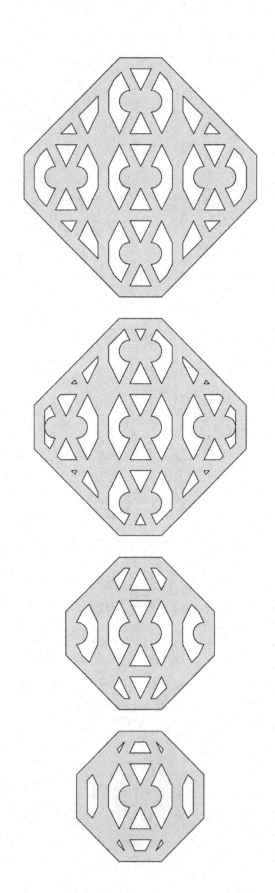

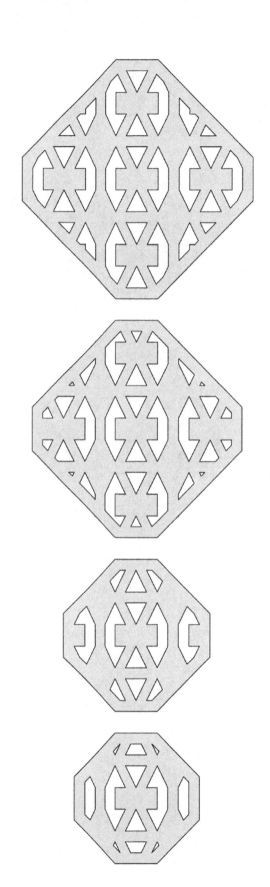

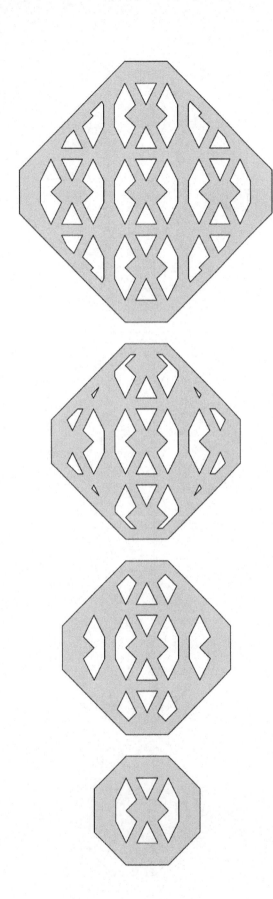
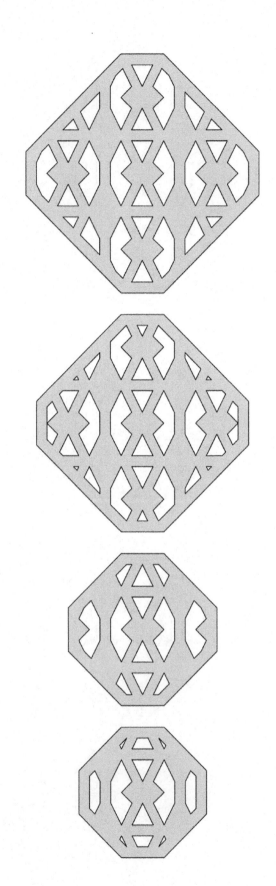

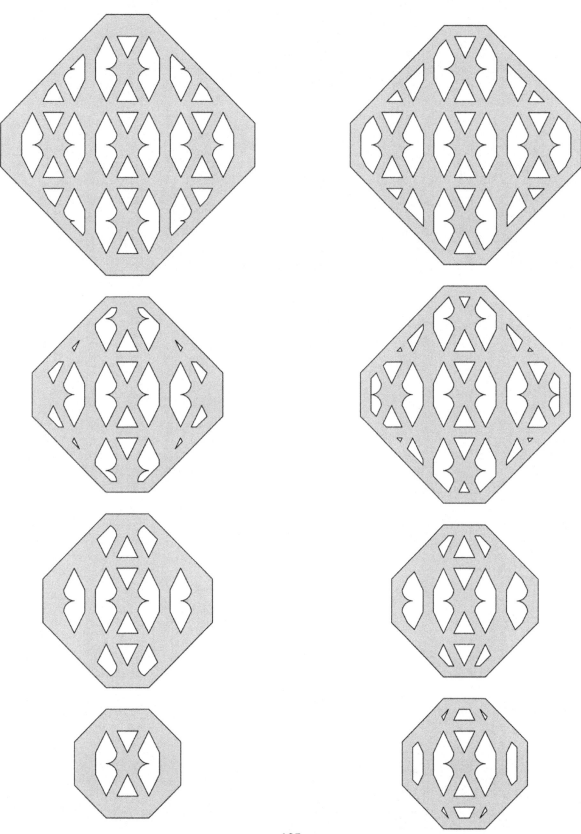

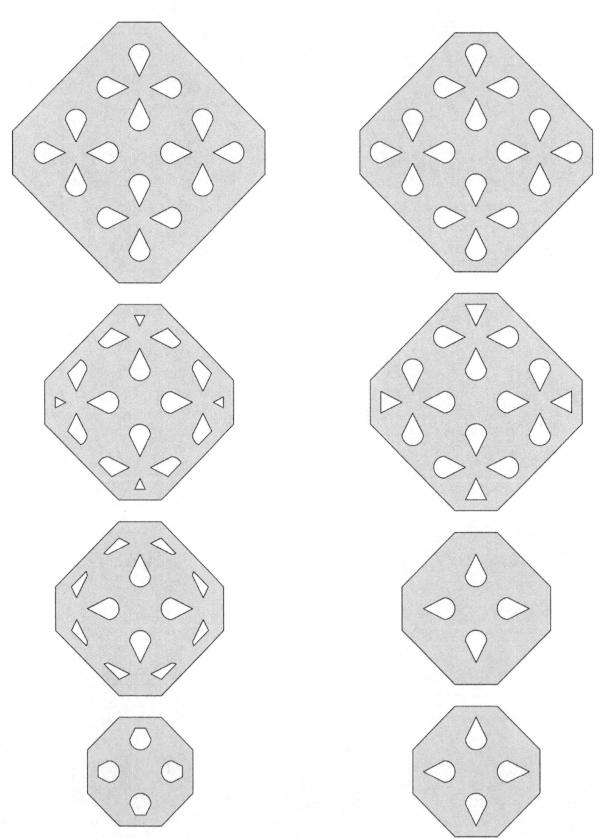

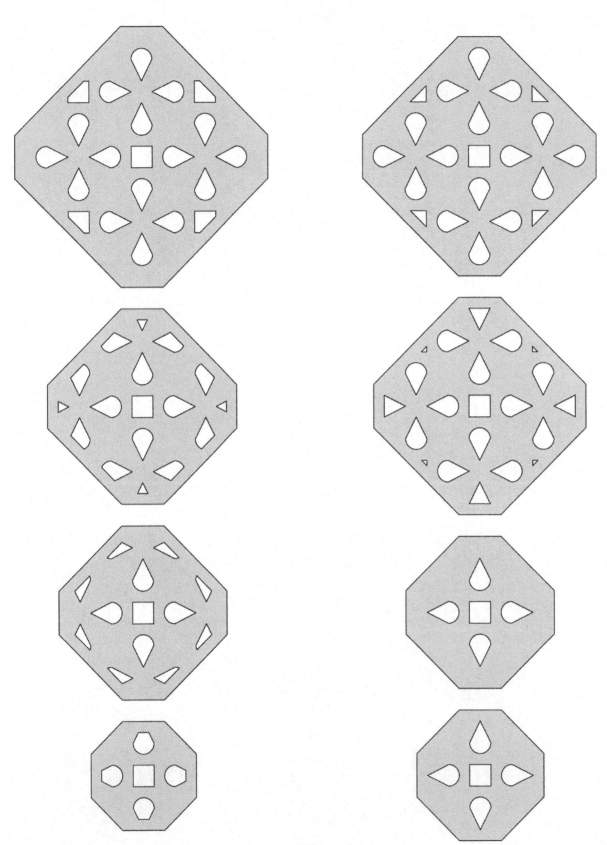

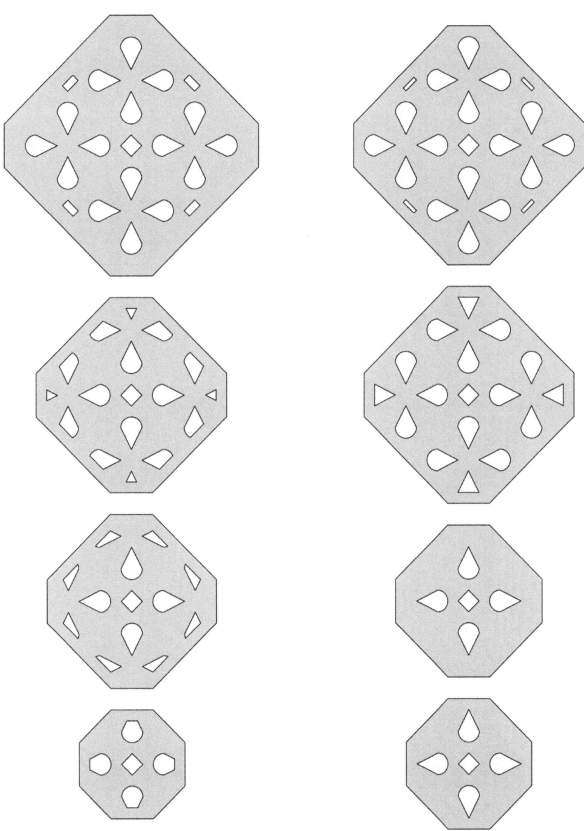

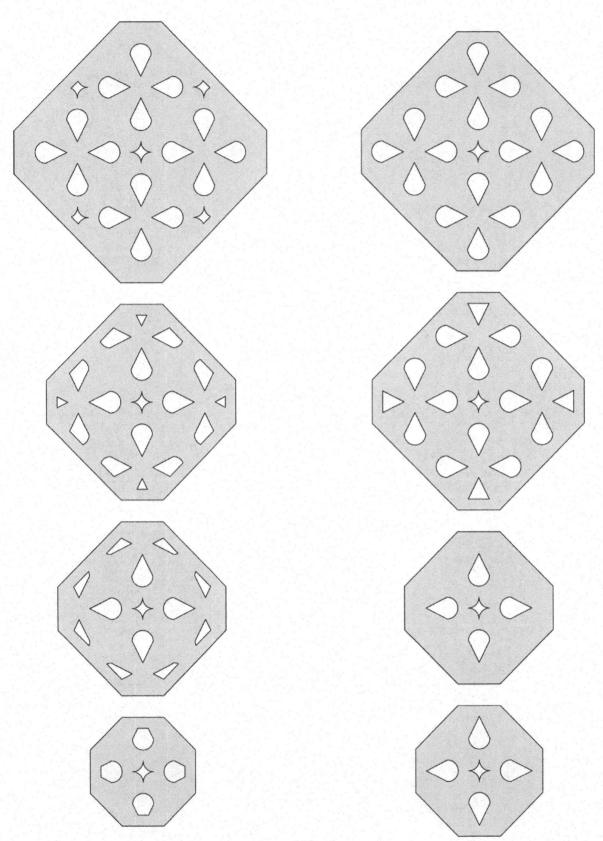

115

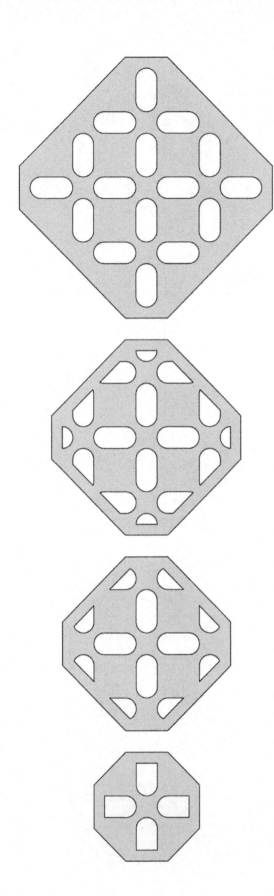
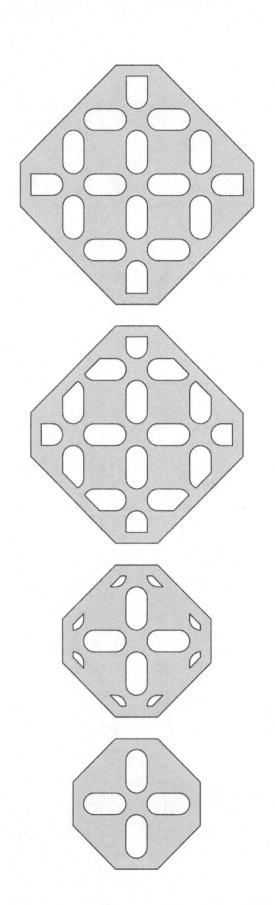

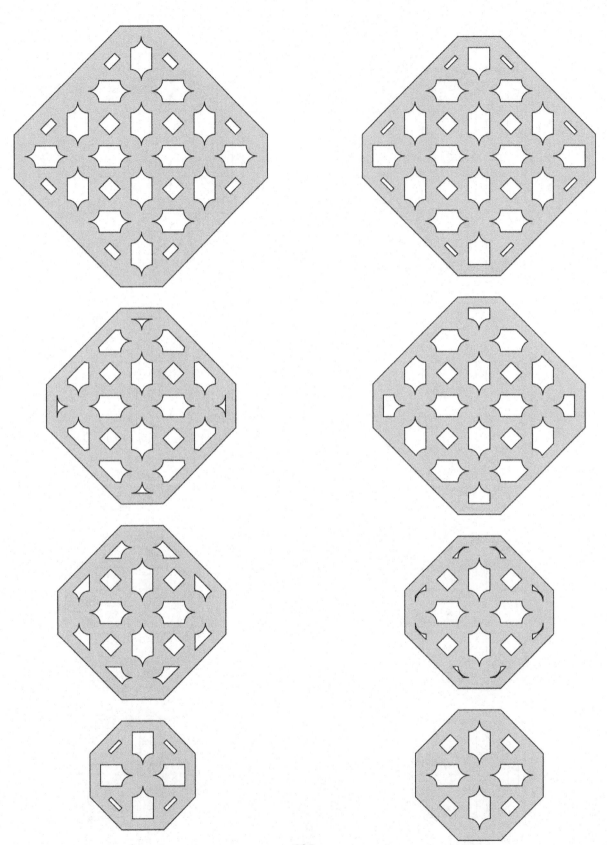

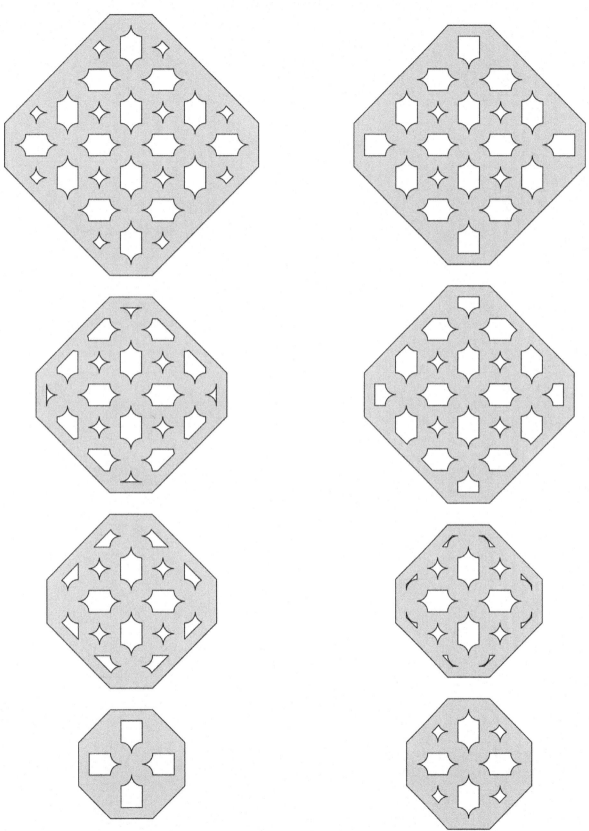

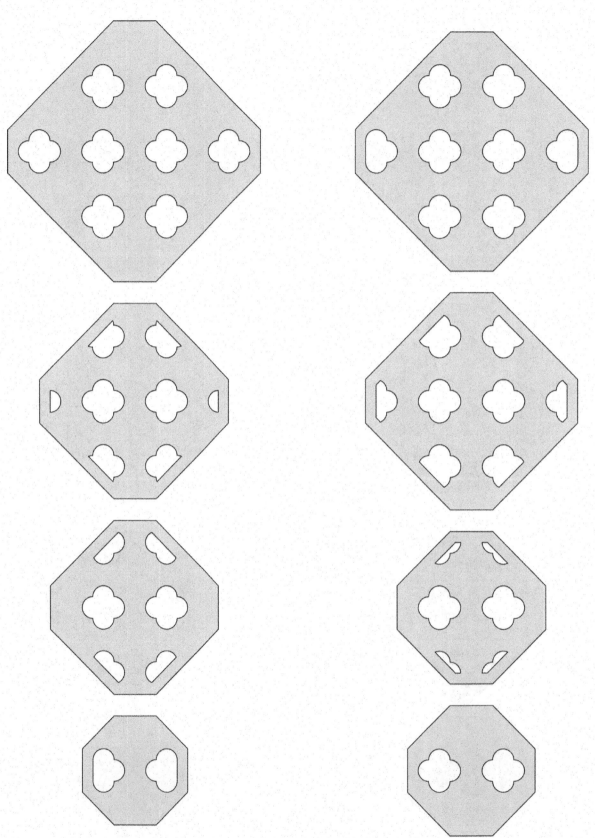

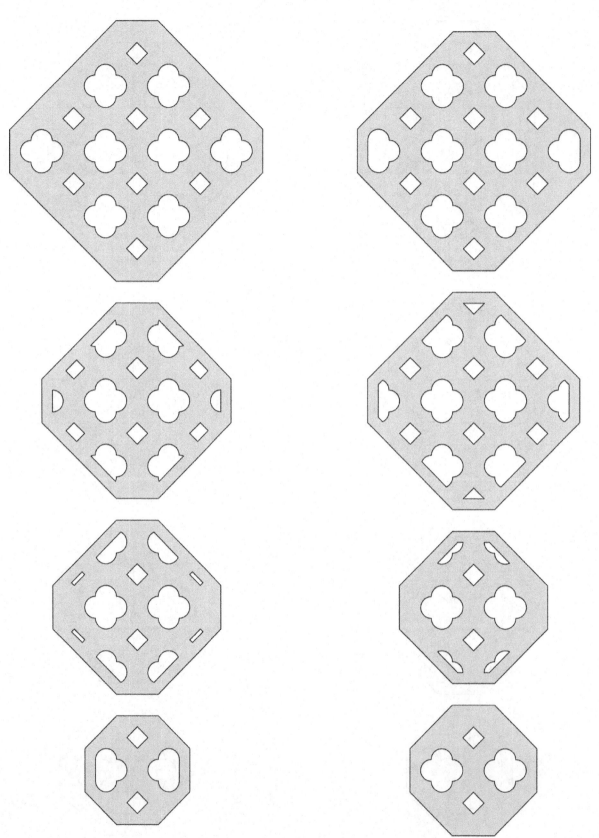

131

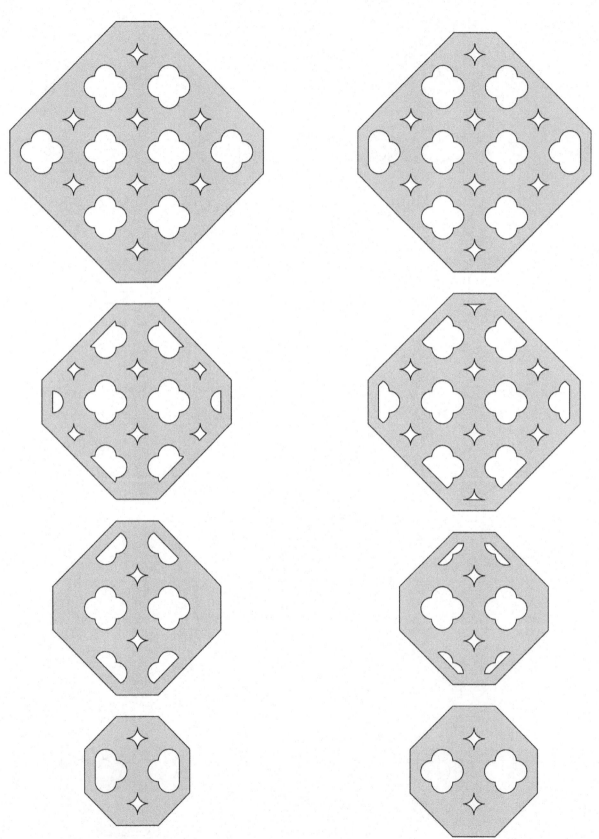

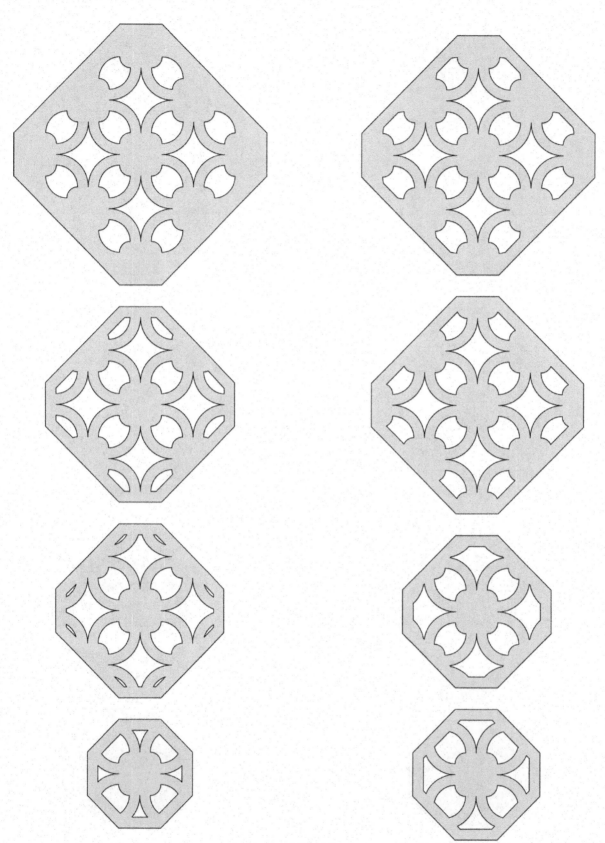

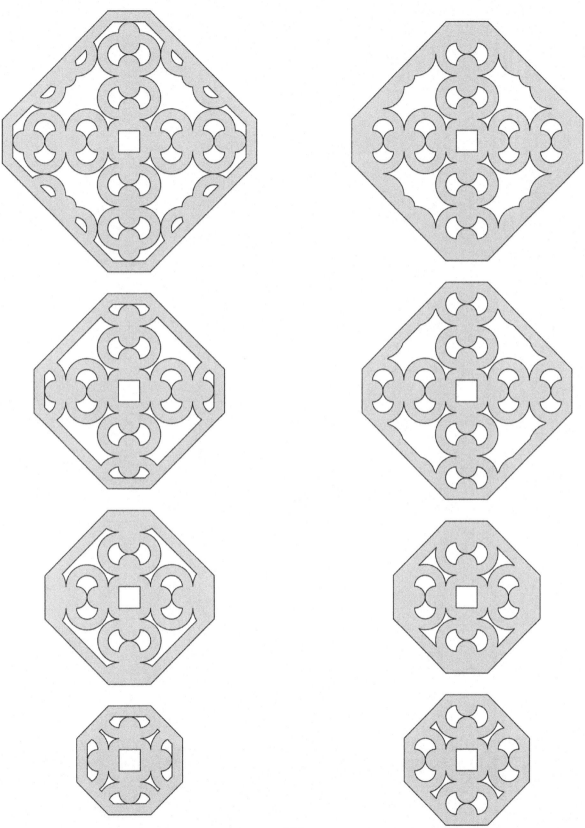

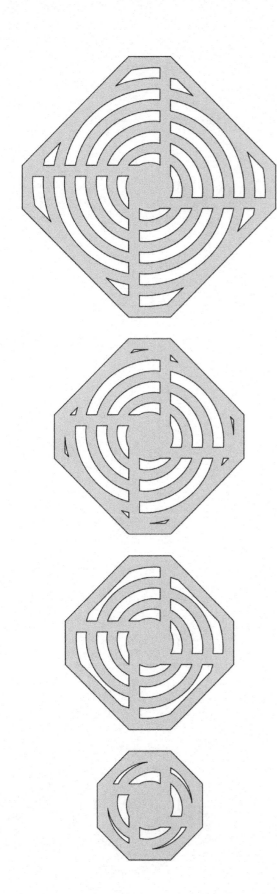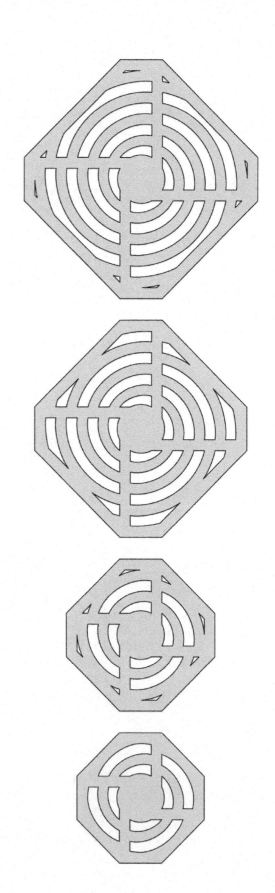

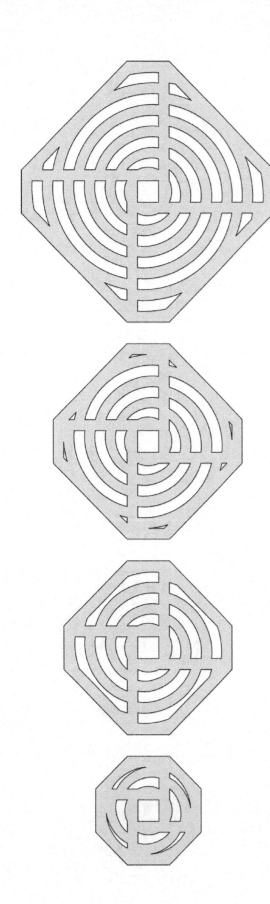

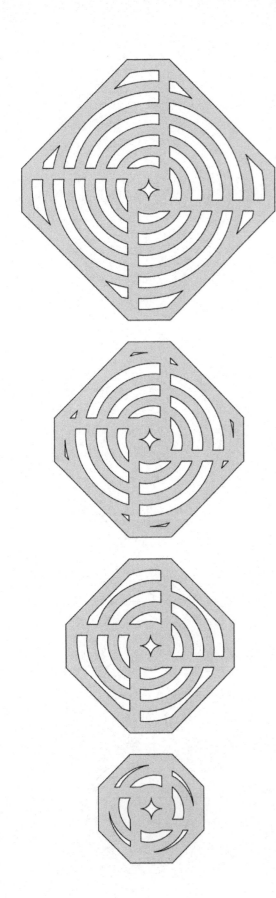

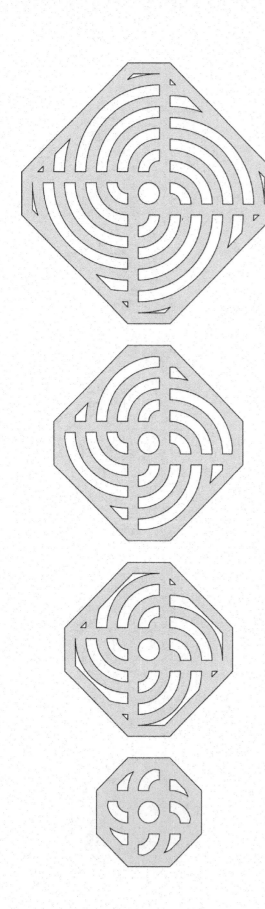

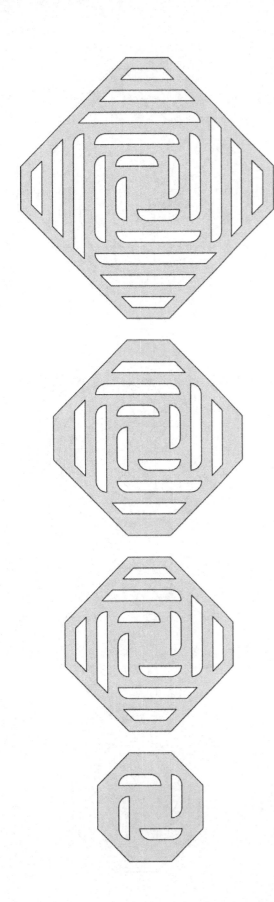

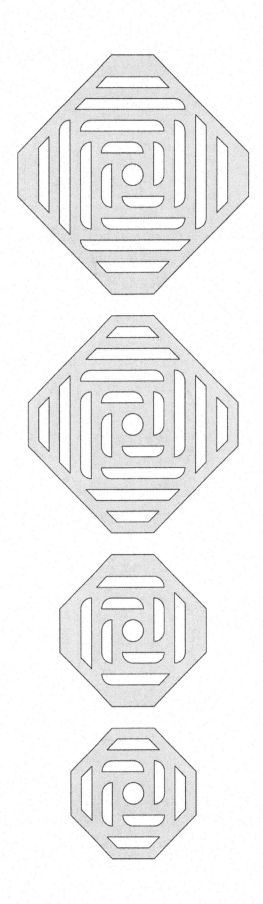

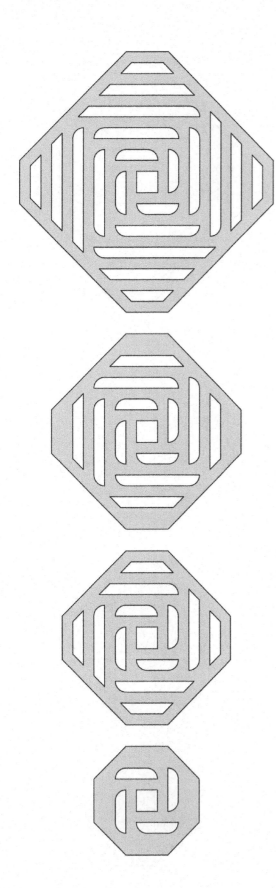

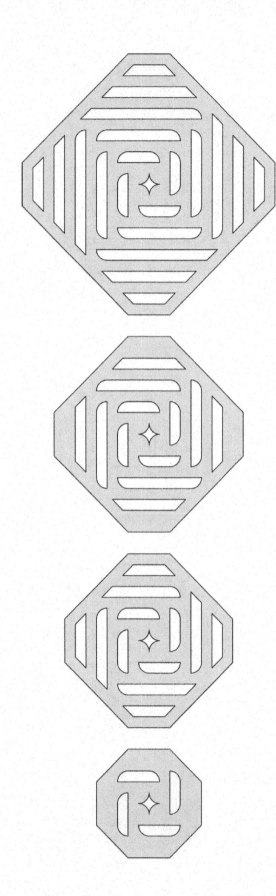

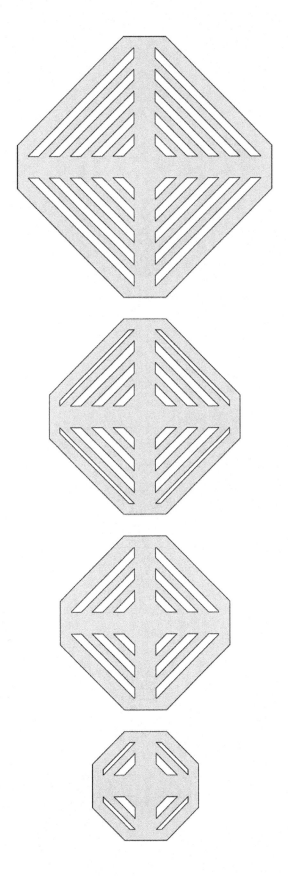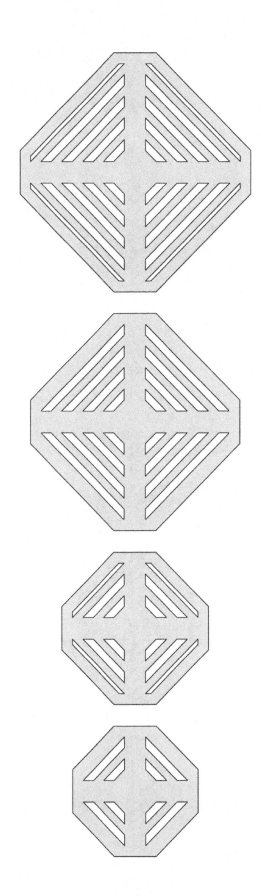

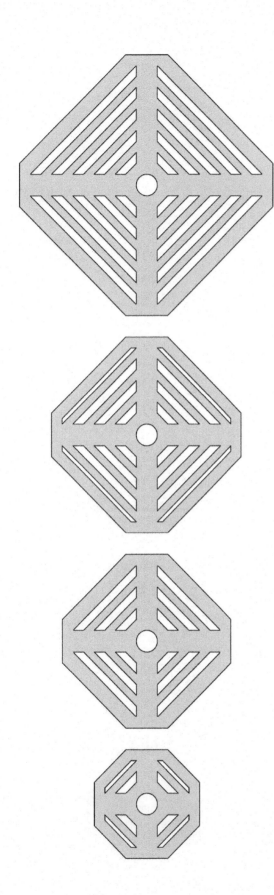
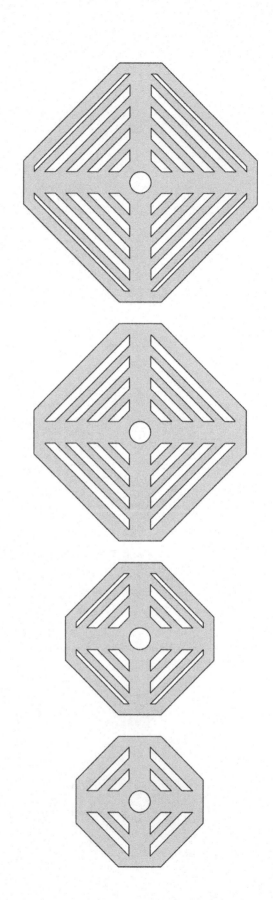

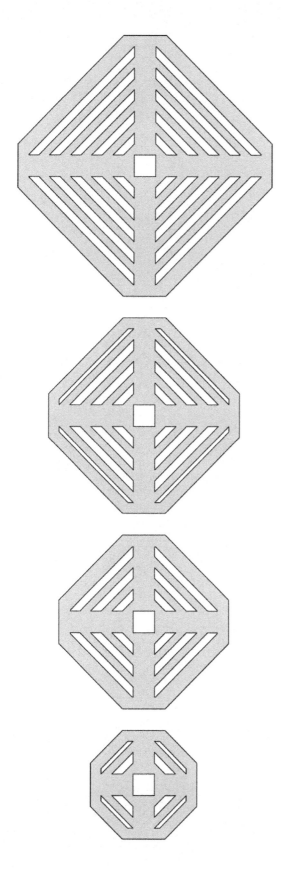
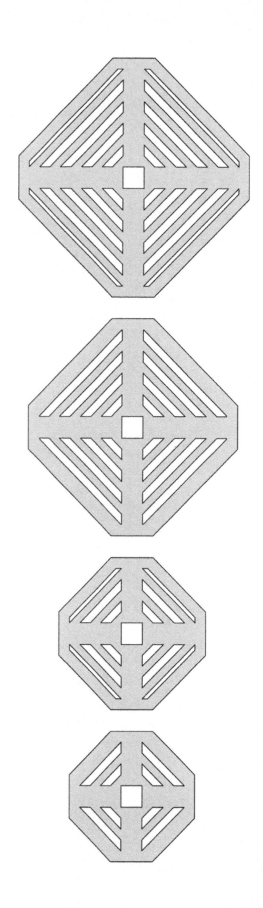

161

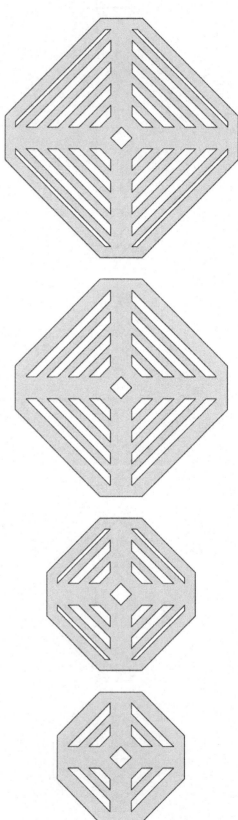

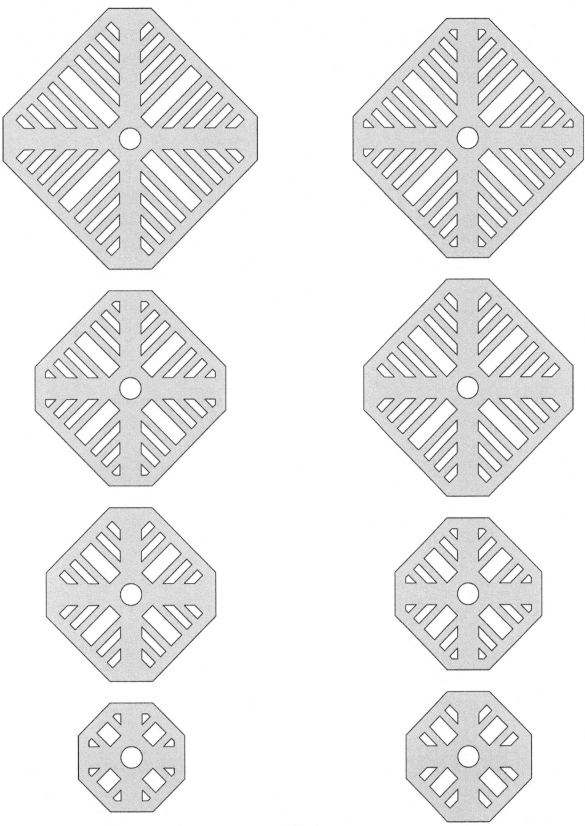

167

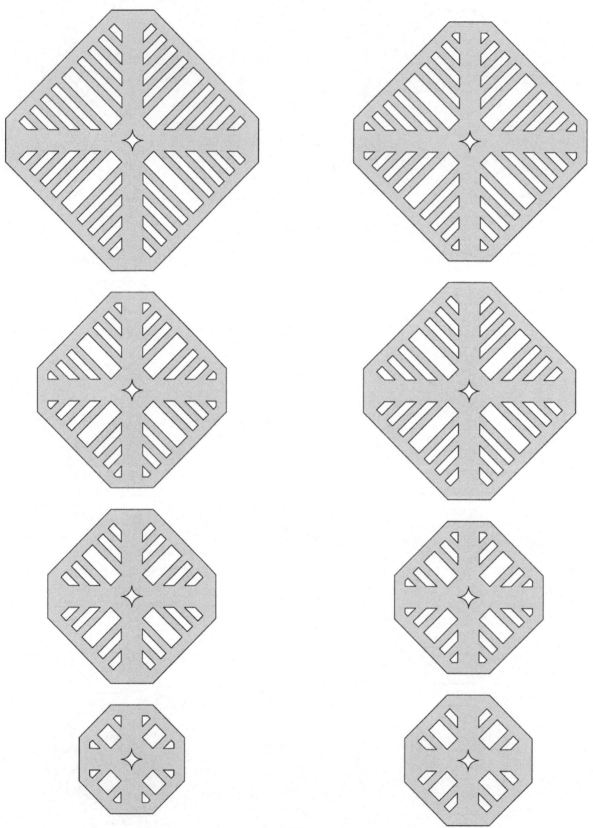